Sound Bible Doctrine

FOR THE

SERVANTS OF

LORD JESUS CHRIST!

Lord Jesus Christ gives us the tools and knowledge we need to serve Him!

Coauthor with *God the Holy Ghost,* **Elder C. Dawse Sloan**

Pastor of THE WAY EVANGELICAL MISSIONARY BAPTIST CHURCH

AuthorHouse™
1663 Liberty Drive
Bloomington, IN 47403
www.authorhouse.com
Phone: 1 (800) 839-8640

Published by AuthorHouse 01/31/2015

ISBN: 978-1-4969-6288-1 (sc)
ISBN: 978-1-4969-6289-8 (e)

Library of Congress Control Number: 2015900282

Any people depicted in stock imagery provided by Thinkstock are models, and such images are being used for illustrative purposes only.
Certain stock imagery © Thinkstock.

This book is printed on acid-free paper.

Because of the dynamic nature of the Internet, any web addresses or links contained in this book may have changed since publication and may no longer be valid. The views expressed in this work are solely those of the author and do not necessarily reflect the views of the publisher, and the publisher hereby disclaims any responsibility for them.

authorHOUSE®

Preface

The most important thing that a believer can do is to read the whole Bible from the beginning to the end, in the order that God the Holy Ghost had mankind to write and organize it.

We cannot mature spiritually without the knowledge of God's holy word that's found in the Bible. Many professing Christians say that they love God, but refuse to take the time and read everything that Holy God has provided in the Bible for us.

God in the person of Lord Jesus Christ has started a relationship with every believer, but in order for that relationship to grow into a closer fellowship with God, we need to learn as much about God that we possibly can, and we do that by reading and studying the Bible.

If we allow God the Holy Ghost/Spirit to lead us and guide us like we should, then and only then will we take the time to read the whole Bible from the beginning to the end, instead of jumping around in the Bible from one place to other places in the Bible. When we take the time to read the whole Bible from the beginning to the end, we begin to see how miraculously the whole Bible ties together, the Old Testament and the New Testament complements one another, and we can't truly understand one without the other.

The Bible tells us everything that we need to know about God, ourselves, and the World that we live in.

All scripture references and verses in this book, except for one scripture and reference from The New Living Bible Translation [*NLT*] are from the King James Version of the Bible [*KJV*].

Contents

Chapter 1: General Information.

THE GOOD NEWS OF LORD JESUS CHRIST

There are some things that every believer needs to know. We need to know that Lord Jesus Christ sacrificed His physical body to provide salvation for us (*believing mankind*).

But, what does that mean? What is salvation?

Salvation is the totally, completely finished work of God in the person of Lord Jesus Christ in providing a bridge or the way for mankind to cross over from a state of condemnation (*spiritual separation from God*), to a state of justification (*spiritual connection with God*).

Mankind (*descendants of Adam*) is born spiritually separated from God, because Adam the created son of God sinned against God in the Garden of Eden, which caused Adam to become spiritually separated from God.

Lord Jesus Christ makes it possible for mankind to get back the relationship with Almighty Holy God that Adam first had before sinning against God. Adam's sin against God caused every human being except Lord Jesus Christ (*does not have a human father*) to be born spiritually separated from God; therefore every one of us is born with a sin nature that is in rebellion against Almighty Holy God.

Therefore whenever we say that Lord Jesus Christ provides Salvation for mankind, we are saying that the spiritual connection that mankind in the person of Adam the created son of God lost is made available again through Lord Jesus Christ.

> The Bible says, "**Romans 6:23 [KJV]** ²³For the wages of sin is death; but the gift of God is eternal life through Jesus Christ our Lord."

The payment for sin is spiritual separation from God (*death*), but the gift of God is spiritual connection (*eternal life*) with God through Lord Jesus Christ.

> The Bible also says, "**Ephesians 2:8 - 9 [KJV]** ⁸For by grace are ye saved through faith; and that not of yourselves: *it* is the gift of God: ⁹Not of works, lest any man should boast."

There's absolutely nothing that we can do to earn our way back to God, every one of us have to trust in Lord Jesus Christ finished work on the cross as our only way of being spiritually connected with God forever.

It was God's idea or decision to provide a bridge for mankind in the person of Lord Jesus Christ, to link spiritually separated mankind spiritually back to Almighty Holy God.

We make that spiritual connection with Almighty Holy God through Saving Faith in Lord Jesus Christ.

Saving Faith in Lord Jesus Christ is when we put our trust in only what Lord Jesus Christ has done on the cross for our salvation.

We call the finished work of Lord Jesus Christ on the cross for our salvation the grace of God.

Whenever mankind is confronted with this truth and we believe it to be true, then God the Holy Ghost performs a miraculous conversion in every one of us who believes.

We call this conversion the baptism of the Holy Ghost. The theological term or word for this conversion is <u>regeneration</u>.

> The Bible says, "**Titus 3:5 [KJV]** ⁵Not by works of righteousness which we have done, but according to his mercy he saved us, by the washing of regeneration, and renewing of the Holy Ghost;"

Regeneration is when God the Holy Ghost changes our disposition or attitude toward God from an enemy of God, to an adopted child of God.

The way that God causes this conversion is by God the Holy Ghost dwelling within every believer to give us the power we need to say no to sin and yes to God.

The indwelling of the Holy Ghost in every believer is also our guarantee that we are no longer enemies of God.

The indwelling of God the Holy Ghost in every believer is our guarantee that we are now the children of God who will be with God for eternity.

Every believer in Lord Jesus Christ should remember and proclaim that:

Lord Jesus Christ was born of a virgin female, who had no sexual relationship with a man before His birth, and He lived a perfect life, without committing any sin.

Lord Jesus Christ is the Son of God and the son of mankind, which means that He is the one and only perfect infinite God – Man, He's one hundred percent human and He's one hundred percent God for eternity; He's equally as much human as He is God!

Lord Jesus Christ died on the cross, and He shed His Holy blood, to pay the sin debt of every one of us who believes in Him. He never got married. He was born of a virgin woman and He experienced physical death as a virgin man.

Lord Jesus Christ was buried in a tomb, and He rose from the dead the third day according to the scriptures.

Lord Jesus Christ was seen alive, by His disciples at different times, for forty days after He rose from the grave.

Lord Jesus Christ disciples watched Him as He ascended into heaven in a Cloud out of their sight, and He sent the Holy Ghost or Holy Spirit on the day of Pentecost that came fifty days after the resurrection of Lord Jesus Christ, to indwell every believer from generation to generation until the church body is completed, and God the Holy Ghost give us the ability to have a close personal relationship with God in the person of Lord Jesus Christ.

Lord Jesus Christ will return someday for all of us who believes in Him, the living and the dead, and we shall be with Him forever.

Notes and Reflection:

What is this Rapture that so many preachers are talking about?

The word Rapture is a term that many Bible scholars and theologians use to explain the scriptures found in the New Testament that informs us that Lord Jesus Christ will return to earth to take all believers who are members of His Church back to Heaven with Him. The biblical definition of the word Rapture is the transporting of all believers that are members of the church body of Lord Jesus Christ from earth to Heaven. <u>See the following scripture references below:</u>

John 14:1 - 3 [KJV] [1]Let not your heart be troubled: ye believe in God, believe also in me. [2]In my Father's house are many mansions: if *it* were not *so*, I would have told you. I go to prepare a place for you. [3]And if I go and prepare a place for you, I will come again, and receive you unto myself; that where I am, there ye may be also.

1 Thessalonians 4:13 - 17 [KJV] [13]But I would not have you to be ignorant, brethren, concerning them which are asleep, that ye sorrow not, even as others which have no hope. [14]For if we believe that Jesus died and rose again, even so them also which sleep in Jesus will God bring with him. [15]For this we say unto you by the word of the Lord, that we which are alive *and* remain unto the coming of the Lord shall not prevent them which are asleep. [16]For the Lord himself shall descend from heaven with a shout, with the voice of the archangel, and with the trump of God: and the dead in Christ shall rise first: [17]Then we which are alive *and* remain shall be caught up together with them in the clouds, to meet the Lord in the air: and so shall we ever be with the Lord.

1 Corinthians 15:51 - 55 [KJV] [51]Behold, I show you a mystery; We shall not all sleep, but we shall all be changed, [52]In a moment, in the twinkling of an eye, at the last trump: for the trumpet shall sound, and the dead shall be raised incorruptible, and we shall be changed. [53]For this corruptible must put on incorruption, and this mortal *must* put on immortality. [54]So when this corruptible shall have put on incorruption, and this mortal shall have put on immortality, then shall be brought to pass the saying that is written, Death is swallowed up in victory. [55]O death, where *is* thy sting? O grave, where *is* thy victory?

Notes and Reflection:

The Christian Sabbath

There is still some confusion about on what days a Christian should be worshipping God. Many professing Christians do not know why we have worship services mainly on Sundays; it's something that they were taught to do when they were little children. Unfortunately because of a failure to read and study the whole Bible, some professing Christian have joined cults that say we should be worshipping on a Saturday, because Saturday (*the seventh day of the week*) is the Sabbath day.

The reason we worship on a Sunday is because Lord Jesus Christ rose from the dead on a Sunday (*the first day of the week*). The Bible says, "**Mark 16:9 [KJV]** ⁹ Now when *Jesus* was risen early the first *day* of the week, he appeared first to Mary Magdalene, out of whom he had cast seven devils." Therefore the first century believers started meeting and preaching on the first day of the week, which is Sunday by our calendars, and the Bible clearly says this, "**Acts 20:7 [KJV]** ⁷ And upon the first *day* of the week, when the disciples came together to break bread, Paul preached unto them, ready to depart on the morrow; and continued his speech until midnight."

Please share this information with other believers, those living under the Law Dispensation was obligated to worship on the Sabbath day which is Saturday by our calendars. We are living under the Dispensation of Grace, and the first century believers made that distinction by choosing to worship on Sunday instead of Saturday.

Notes and Reflection:

Chapter 2: Apologetics.

Does God choose believers or do believers choose God?

According to the Bible, because of the total depravity of mankind, God has to choose us (*mankind*), we cannot choose God, nor do we desire to have a relationship with God. The Bible says, "**Jeremiah 17:9 [KJV]** ⁹The heart *is* deceitful above all *things,* and desperately wicked: who can know it?"

> **John 3:19 [KJV]** ¹⁹And this is the condemnation, that light is come into the world, and men loved darkness rather than light, because their deeds were evil.

Apart from God or separated from God, the Bible describes mankind as being totally corrupt, wicked, ungodly, evil, and deceitful.

> **Genesis 6:4 - 7 [KJV]** ⁴There were giants in the earth in those days; and also after that, when the sons of God came in unto the daughters of men, and they bare *children* to them, the same *became* mighty men which *were* of old, men of renown. ⁵And God saw that the wickedness of man was great in the earth, and *that* every imagination of the thoughts of his heart *was* only evil continually. ⁶And it repented the LORD that he had made man on the earth, and it grieved him at his heart. ⁷And the LORD said, I will destroy man whom I have created from the face of the earth; both man, and beast, and the creeping thing, and the fowls of the air; for it repenteth me that I have made them.

> **Genesis 8:20 - 22 [KJV]** ²⁰And Noah builded an altar unto the LORD; and took of every clean beast, and of every clean fowl, and offered burnt offerings on the altar. ²¹And the LORD smelled a sweet savour; and the LORD said in his heart, I will not again curse the ground any more for man's sake; for the imagination of man's heart *is* evil from his youth; neither will I again smite any more every thing living, as I have done. ²²While the earth remaineth, seedtime and harvest, and cold and heat, and summer and winter, and day and night shall not cease.

There are many people in the World today that believe that mankind is basically good, but circumstances cause a good person to become bad. Lord Jesus Christ says that no one is good, except God! **Matthew 19:16 - 17 [KJV]** ¹⁶And, behold, one came and said unto him, Good Master, what good thing shall I do, that I may have eternal life? ¹⁷And he said unto him, Why callest thou me good? *there is* none good but one, *that is,* God: but if thou wilt enter into life, keep the commandments.

Apart from God or separated from God mankind cannot keep the Ten Commandments because the commandments are perfect and we (*mankind*) are imperfect.

Ephesians 1:3 - 7 [KJV] ³Blessed *be* the God and Father of our Lord Jesus Christ, who hath blessed us with all spiritual blessings in heavenly *places* in Christ: ⁴According as he hath chosen us in him before the foundation of the world, that we should be holy and without blame before him in love: ⁵Having predestinated us unto the adoption of children by Jesus Christ to himself, according to the good pleasure of his will, ⁶To the praise of the glory of his grace, wherein he hath made us accepted in the beloved. ⁷In whom we have redemption through his blood, the forgiveness of sins, according to the riches of his grace;

Almighty Holy God is the one who chooses us (*mankind*).

Lord Jesus Christ says, "**John 6:44 [KJV]** ⁴⁴No man can come to me, except the Father which hath sent me draw him: and I will raise him up at the last day."

God does the choosing and believing mankind simply does the receiving. This is where our freewill comes into play, even though God provides salvation for us and chooses whom He will to receive salvation by giving believers the kind of faith that is needed for believers to make the right decision; we (*believers*) still have to freely choose to receive the salvation that God has provided. It's like a marriage proposal when a man see a woman that he wants to marry and he starts dating her to make her like him, then he pops the question and it's up to her to say yes or no to marry him.

Self-righteousness is a component of mankind's inherited sin nature. Apart from God or separated from God, unbelievers see nothing wrong with passing judgment upon God. Some people say, "*How can a God of love allow innocent children to be murdered*" or "*It's unfair for God to choose some people and not all*".

The Bible says, "**Romans 9:20 - 24 [KJV]** ²⁰Nay but, O man, who art thou that repliest against God? Shall the thing formed say to him that formed *it*, Why hast thou made me thus? ²¹Hath not the potter power over the clay, of the same lump to make one vessel unto honour, and another unto dishonour? ²²*What* if God, willing to show *his* wrath, and to make his power known, endured with much longsuffering the vessels of wrath fitted to destruction: ²³And that he might make known the riches of his glory on the vessels of mercy, which he had afore prepared unto glory, ²⁴Even us, whom he hath called, not of the Jews only, but also of the Gentiles?"

The proper response of mankind to God's choosing some and not all of mankind to spend eternity with God should be, "*Praise God for choosing some people, because all deserve to perish into the Lake of Fire for eternity*". But even still a self-righteous selfish mind will say, "*If God doesn't save all, then God shouldn't save any*". The bottom line is this, being God means that God can do whatever God wants to do, and God does not have to justify Himself to wicked mankind!

Notes and Reflection:

Law and/or Grace, which is it?

There is a false doctrine that's been in the World ever since the first century when the Church or The Way, was started by Lord Jesus Christ. The false doctrine says that if a person believes in Lord Jesus Christ for salvation, they have to also live according to the Mosaic Law that was given to the nation of Israel.

According to Dispensationalist the Bible is divided into seven dispensations. They say that a dispensation is a period of time in which God deals with mankind's responsibility and sin in a particular way. They also say that the first dispensation is **Innocence,** which occurred in the Garden of Eden before Adam disobeyed God. After Innocence came **Conscience** which occurred when Adam ate the forbidden fruit of the tree of the knowledge of good and evil. After Conscience **Human Government,** which occurred after Noah built the ark and God flooded the earth. After Human Government **Promise** which occurred when God promised Abram (*Abraham*) land and descendants. After Promise **Law** which occurred when God gave Moses the Ten Commandments on Mount Sinai. After Law **Grace** which occurred after Lord Jesus Christ's physical death on the cross, burial, resurrection, and ascension back to Heaven. The last dispensation coming after Grace is **Kingdom** (*The Millennium*), which will occur after the end of the Great Tribulation and last for a thousand years.

There is no such thing as, *"What was there before God?"* Time does not precede God, because God created time. God controls time and what happens during time.

During the dispensation of Law, the Law was given to reveal the sinful nature of mankind; as a mirror for us (*mankind*) to see how we (*mankind*) apart from God or separated from God are rebellious against God! If imperfect mankind could keep or do the perfect commandments of God, then it would be a way of showing love to one another.

> The Bible says, "**Ephesians 3:1 - 7 [KJV]** ¹For this cause I Paul, the prisoner of Jesus Christ for you Gentiles, ²If ye have heard of the dispensation of the grace of God which is given me to you-ward: ³How that by revelation he made known unto me the mystery; (as I wrote afore in few words, ⁴Whereby, when ye read, ye may understand my knowledge in the mystery of Christ) ⁵Which in other ages was not made known unto the sons of men, as it is now revealed unto his holy apostles and prophets by the Spirit; ⁶That the Gentiles should be fellowheirs, and of the same body, and partakers of his promise in Christ by the gospel: ⁷Whereof I was made a minister, according to the gift of the grace of God given unto me by the effectual working of his power."

Now that Lord Jesus Christ has brought in the dispensation of Grace by His death on the cross, burial, resurrection, and ascension back to the throne of God, we are supposed to live on a higher plane than the Law that was given during the Law dispensation. We are supposed to allow Lord Jesus Christ to produce love (*the fruit of the Spirit*) in us and through us.

Romans 13:8 [KJV] ⁸Owe no man any thing, but to love one another: for he that loveth another hath fulfilled the law.

Galatians 5:14 [KJV] ¹⁴For all the law is fulfilled in one word, *even* in this; Thou shalt love thy neighbour as thyself.

The Bible says, "**Galatians 5:22 - 25 [KJV]** ²²But the fruit of the Spirit is love, joy, peace, longsuffering, gentleness, goodness, faith, ²³Meekness, temperance: against such there is no law. ²⁴And they that are Christ's have crucified the flesh with the affections and lusts. ²⁵If we live in the Spirit, let us also walk in the Spirit."

Lord Jesus Christ says, "**John 15:1 - 8 [KJV]** ¹I am the true vine, and my Father is the husbandman. ²Every branch in me that beareth not fruit he taketh away: and every *branch* that beareth fruit, he purgeth it, that it may bring forth more fruit. ³Now ye are clean through the word which I have spoken unto you. ⁴Abide in me, and I in you. As the branch cannot bear fruit of itself, except it abide in the vine; no more can ye, except ye abide in me. ⁵I am the vine, ye *are* the branches: He that abideth in me, and I in him, the same bringeth forth much fruit: for without me ye can do nothing. ⁶If a man abide not in me, he is cast forth as a branch, and is withered; and men gather them, and cast *them* into the fire, and they are burned. ⁷If ye abide in me, and my words abide in you, ye shall ask what ye will, and it shall be done unto you. ⁸Herein is my Father glorified, that ye bear much fruit; so shall ye be my disciples."

Every dispensation, even **Kingdom** (*The Millennium*) to come, where people will be born into a perfect God fearing World for a thousand years without the devil, once Satan the devil is released into the World again, many of the people will join sides with the devil against God, which proves that apart from God or separated from God the total depravity of mankind.

The Law condemns us (*mankind*) to death (*spiritual separation from God for eternity*) but Grace gives us life (*a spiritual connection to God for eternity*). We cannot have both at the same time, if we say that we have to put our faith in Lord Jesus Christ and also keep the Law to be saved, then we are saying that Lord Jesus Christ's finished work on the cross is not enough to save mankind. Whenever a person combines faith in Lord Jesus Christ and the keeping of the Law (*Ten Commandments or any other set of rules, etc.*) for salvation, then he or she is saying that God is a liar; he or she is saying that what Lord Jesus Christ did on the cross is not enough, and by doing that, he or she is rejecting the way that God says we have to be saved.

Whenever we do it our way instead of God's way, we have not accepted the free gift of eternal life that Lord Jesus Christ finished work on the cross provides; we are still trying to earn our way into God's presence (*Heaven*) for eternity with our so-called good deeds, but the Law keep condemning our deeds, because our motive for doing the so-called good deeds are wrong.

Lord Jesus Christ is the grace of God, and mankind's salvation is obtained by believing what God says concerning the finished work of Lord Jesus Christ on the cross. God says that, **"Romans 6:23 [KJV]** [23]For the wages of sin *is* death; but the gift of God *is* eternal life through Jesus Christ our Lord."

> "**Ephesians 2:8 - 9 [KJV]** [8]For by grace are ye saved through faith; and that not of yourselves: *it is* the gift of God: [9]Not of works, lest any man should boast."

Salvation is a transaction between a person (*a sinner*) and Holy God, not between a sinner and another sinner. Stop trying to impress other people for salvation.

> The Bible says, "**2 Corinthians 5:19 - 21 [KJV]** [19]To wit, that God was in Christ, reconciling the world unto himself, not imputing their trespasses unto them; and hath committed unto us the word of reconciliation. [20]Now then we are ambassadors for Christ, as though God did beseech *you* by us: we pray *you* in Christ's stead, be ye reconciled to God. [21]For he hath made him *to be* sin for us, who knew no sin; that we might be made the righteousness of God in him."

The bottom line is this, if we say or believe somebody else who says that a person has to believe that Lord Jesus Christ died on the cross for our sins, but we have to do this and that also to be saved and keep our salvation, then we are believing in a false doctrine that originated from Satan the devil through mankind that's sending many people to the Lake of Fire after they die. Salvation or God's grace towards mankind is Lord Jesus Christ physical death on the cross (*the shedding of His holy blood*), burial, resurrection, ascension into Heaven, return in the future, and nothing else added.

Notes and Reflection:

Once saved always saved or can we lose our salvation?

There is a division among professing Christians in the local churches about salvation. Some believe that a person can lose their salvation after being saved and others believe that once we are saved, we are always saved.

The way that a person view salvation will affect the way he or she interprets scripture. A carnal mind will interpret scripture differently from a spiritual discerning mind.

The Bible tells us that salvation is a gift, "**Romans 6:23 [KJV]** ²³For the wages of sin *is* death; but the gift of God *is* eternal life through Jesus Christ our Lord."

Ephesians 2:8 - 9 [KJV] ⁸For by grace are ye saved through faith; and that not of yourselves: *it is* the gift of God: ⁹Not of works, lest any man should boast.

The dictionary says that a gift is "*something given voluntarily without payment in return, as to honor a person or an occasion or to provide assistance; present.*"

The question is, "*How can someone unearned something he or she never earned to start with?*" If a person believes that he or she can unearned a gift or give back a gift, then that person never truly accepted the gift. All gifts have to be accepted freely without charge or payment, otherwise it is not a gift.

We need to first talk about the <u>blood</u>, because it is the Holy shed <u>blood</u> of Lord Jesus Christ that actually saves us.

The Bible say, "**Leviticus 17:11 - 14 [KJV]** ¹¹For the life of the flesh *is* in the blood: and I have given it to you upon the altar to make an atonement for your souls: for it *is* the blood *that* maketh an atonement for the soul. ¹²Therefore I said unto the children of Israel, No soul of you shall eat blood, neither shall any stranger that sojourneth among you eat blood. ¹³And whatsoever man *there be* of the children of Israel, or of the strangers that sojourn among you, which hunteth and catcheth any beast or fowl that may be eaten; he shall even pour out the blood thereof, and cover it with dust. ¹⁴For *it is* the life of all flesh; the blood of it *is* for the life thereof: therefore I said unto the children of Israel, Ye shall eat the blood of no manner of flesh: for the life of all flesh *is* the blood thereof: whosoever eateth it shall be cut off."

Romans 3:22 - 26 [KJV] ²²Even the righteousness of God *which is* by faith of Jesus Christ unto all and upon all them that believe: for there is no difference: ²³For all have sinned, and come short of the glory of God; ²⁴Being justified freely by his grace through the redemption that is in Christ Jesus: ²⁵Whom God hath set forth *to be* a propitiation through faith in his blood, to declare his righteousness for the remission of sins that are past, through the forbearance of God; ²⁶To declare, *I say*, at this time his righteousness: that he might be just, and the justifier of him which believeth in Jesus.

The next important element of salvation is Faith. The Bible has a lot to say about faith.

The Bible says, "**Habakkuk 2:4 [KJV]** ⁴Behold, his soul *which* is lifted up is not upright in him: but the just shall live by his faith."

Romans 1:16 - 17 [KJV] ¹⁶For I am not ashamed of the gospel of Christ: for it is the power of God unto salvation to every one that believeth; to the Jew first, and also to the Greek. ¹⁷For therein is the righteousness of God revealed from faith to faith: as it is written, The just shall live by faith.

Galatians 3:9 - 11 [KJV] ⁹So then they which be of faith are blessed with faithful Abraham. ¹⁰For as many as are of the works of the law are under the curse: for it is written, Cursed *is* every one that continueth not in all things which are written in the book of the law to do them. ¹¹But that no man is justified by the law in the sight of God, *it is* evident: for, The just shall live by faith.

Hebrews 10:37 - 39 [KJV] ³⁷For yet a little while, and he that shall come will come, and will not tarry. ³⁸Now the just shall live by faith: but if *any man* draw back, my soul shall have no pleasure in him. ³⁹But we are not of them who draw back unto perdition; but of them that believe to the saving of the soul.

The dictionary says that faith is "*confidence or trust in a person or thing.*"

The scripture is talking about having faith in Lord Jesus Christ first for the gift of eternal life (*He saved us from the Lake of Fire*). The scripture is also talking about faith in Lord Jesus Christ to live the Christian life through us. We have to depend on Lord Jesus Christ to keep us from sinning, the only life we know how to live, is the life of a sinner.

The Bible says, "**Romans 5:8 - 11 [KJV]** ⁸But God commendeth his love toward us, in that, while we were yet sinners, Christ died for us. ⁹Much more then, being now justified by his blood, we shall be saved from wrath through him. ¹⁰For if, when we were enemies, we were reconciled to God by the death of his Son, much more, being reconciled, we shall be saved by his life. ¹¹And not only *so*, but we also joy in God through our Lord Jesus Christ, by whom we have now received the atonement." (*Present tense*)

The Bible tells us that Lord Jesus Christ said, "**John 14:12 - 15 [KJV]** ¹²Verily, verily, I say unto you, He that believeth on me, the works that I do shall he do also; and greater *works* than these shall he do; because I go unto my Father. ¹³And whatsoever ye shall ask in my name, that will I do, that the Father may be glorified in the Son. ¹⁴If ye shall ask any thing in my name, I will do *it*. ¹⁵If ye love me, keep my commandments."

Out of gratitude and love for Lord Jesus Christ because He has saved us, we allow Lord Jesus Christ to use us as His instruments in the World today to do good works through us and to keep us from sinning against God. We do it because we are **saved**, not to be **saved** or to keep our salvation!

<u>Creation or Evolution?</u> (*The two cannot exist together*)

Almighty Holy God has revealed to us through His holy written word that's found in the Bible, how mankind came into being. Holy God is the creator of the heavens and the earth, and also mankind.

> The Bible says, "**Genesis 2:1 - 3 [KJV]** ¹Thus the heavens and the earth were finished, and all the host of them. ²And on the seventh day God ended his work which he had made; and he rested on the seventh day from all his work which he had made. ³And God blessed the seventh day, and sanctified it: because that in it he had rested from all his work which God created and made."

> **Genesis 2:7 [KJV]** ⁷And the LORD God formed man *of* the dust of the ground, and breathed into his nostrils the breath of life; and man became a living soul.

The theory of evolution assumes that all life on earth began from a single living cell, but does not explain where the living cell comes from. TTOE (*the theory of evolution*) also assumes that lightning or some kind of explosion (*the big bang theory*) <u>could</u> have caused the various chemicals of the earth to combine in a way that formed the first living cell from which all life forms on the earth exist today.

TTOE claims that mankind has evolved from a primitive state of being to the state of being that we are today, but there is no evidence of such claims, nor is mankind evolving beyond where we are.

An archaeologist, who by the Will of God became a Christian, wrote a book explaining how a certain individual took the skull of a human being and the jaw bone of a gorilla, put them together and used that to prove their theory of the existence of cavemen.

If we look at TTOE with a discerning spirit from a spiritual point of view, then we can clearly see the spiritual battle that Satan the devil is waging against Almighty Holy God, to keep mankind separated from God.

The school system in America was started or set up by Christians that came to America, so that their children would know and learn about Almighty Holy God.

It's truly amazing how things have changed; now evolution is taught in our school system and the Bible, Prayer, or anything pertaining to God, is not permitted in the public schools anymore.

The carnal mind of the unsaved person, regardless of how intellectual he or she might be, is unable to recognize the battle that the devil is waging against God for the souls of mankind.

Satan the devil has been using the theory of evolution to cause many people to <u>disbelieve</u> in the existence of God. Many individuals have become an atheist because of their belief in the theory of the evolution of mankind.

The theory of evolution along with the anti-Christ atmosphere of the United States of America that we are living in, has caused many individuals to choose the path of self-destruction (*by eventually spending eternity in the Lake of Fire*), because they have chosen to believe the lies of the devil. The theory of the evolution of mankind is first of all a theory, there is no facts or proof to confirm it, don't believe it, it is a satanic lie!

Notes and Reflection:

Annihilation or Life after Death

Atheist believes that when a person experience physical death, he or she is gone forever; they believe that there is no life after death.

The Bible says, "**Psalms 14:1 [KJV]** ¹ The fool hath said in his heart, *There is* no God. They are corrupt, they have done abominable works, *there is* none that doeth good."

Psalms 53:1 [KJV] ¹ The fool hath said in his heart, *There is* no God. Corrupt are they, and have done abominable iniquity: *there is* none that doeth good.

Whenever the Bible says the same (*almost exact words*) thing twice, it has to be important. If we ever wondered about the biblical definition of an atheist, I think we have it here in those two above scripture references (*Psalms 14:1 & 53:1*).

Lord Jesus Christ responded to those individuals in the first century that did not believe in a person becoming alive again after experiencing physical death; the Bible says, "**Mark 12:18 - 27 [KJV]** ¹⁸Then come unto him the Sadducees, which say there is no resurrection; and they asked him, saying, ¹⁹Master, Moses wrote unto us, If a man's brother die, and leave *his* wife *behind him*, and leave no children, that his brother should take his wife, and raise up seed unto his brother. ²⁰Now there were seven brethren: and the first took a wife, and dying left no seed. ²¹And the second took her, and died, neither left he any seed: and the third likewise. ²²And the seven had her, and left no seed: last of all the woman died also. ²³In the resurrection therefore, when they shall rise, whose wife shall she be of them? for the seven had her to wife. ²⁴And Jesus answering said unto them, Do ye not therefore err, because ye know not the scriptures, neither the power of God? ²⁵For when they shall rise from the dead, they neither marry, nor are given in marriage; but are as the angels which are in heaven. ²⁶And as touching the dead, that they rise: have ye not read in the book of Moses, how in the bush God spake unto him, saying, I *am* the God of Abraham, and the God of Isaac, and the God of Jacob? ²⁷He is not the God of the dead, but the God of the living: ye therefore do greatly err."

The Bible also says, "**Revelation 20:11 - 15 [KJV]** ¹¹And I saw a great white throne, and him that sat on it, from whose face the earth and the heaven fled away; and there was found no place for them. ¹²And I saw the dead, small and great, stand before God; and the books were opened: and another book was opened, which is *the book* of life: and the dead were judged out of those things which were written in the books, according to their works. ¹³And the sea gave up the dead which were in it; and death and hell delivered up the dead which were in them: and they were judged every man according to their works. ¹⁴And death and hell were cast into the lake of fire. This is the second death. ¹⁵And whosoever was not found written in the book of life was cast into the lake of fire."

The Bible has a lot to say about life after death.

According to the Bible every person that ever lived will be resurrected and/or changed to live in Heaven with God for eternity or to be casted in the Lake of Fire for eternity. Many of us chose to live in Heaven with God for eternity by accepting Lord Jesus Christ as our Savior, and those who haven't already done so, need to choose Lord Jesus Christ as their Savior; otherwise those who reject or refuse to accept the free gift of eternal life in Heaven with God that Lord Jesus Christ has made available to mankind, will spend eternity in the Lake of Fire.

Do not believe the lie that the devil has convinced the atheists to believe, saying that, *"once you're dead, you're done."* Do the research and see for yourself how the Bible prophecies have been fulfilled. The Bible predicted the first coming of Lord Jesus Christ to earth and the Bible has also predicted that Lord Jesus Christ is coming back to earth again. Lord Jesus Christ is the only one who can keep us from being casted into the Lake of Fire (*torment for eternity*).

Annihilation is a lie! Every human being will live forever in Heaven or in the Lake of Fire. Satan the devil is a liar and will be casted into the Lake of Fire for eternity; do not let that liar trick you into going into the Lake of Fire with him!

Notes and Reflection:

Good Friday or Good Wednesday?

Let's go to the Bible to figure out exactly when our Lord and Savior Jesus Christ died on the cross for our salvation.

The Bible says, "**Matthew 12:38 - 40 [KJV]** [38]Then certain of the scribes and of the Pharisees answered, saying, Master, we would see a sign from thee. [39]But he answered and said unto them, An evil and adulterous generation seeketh after a sign; and there shall no sign be given to it, but the sign of the prophet Jonas: [40]For as Jonas was three days and three nights in the whale's belly; so shall the Son of man be three days and three nights in the heart of the earth."

Notice from the scripture text that Lord Jesus Christ is talking about three whole days, not half of days, because He clearly says three days and three nights. Let's go back to the Bible to see God's definition of a day.

The Bible says, "**Genesis 1:3 - 8 [KJV]** [3]And God said, Let there be light: and there was light. [4]And God saw the light, that *it was* good: and God divided the light from the darkness. [5]And God called the light Day, and the darkness he called Night. And the evening and the morning were the first day. [6]And God said, Let there be a firmament in the midst of the waters, and let it divide the waters from the waters. [7]And God made the firmament, and divided the waters which *were* under the firmament from the waters which *were* above the firmament: and it was so. [8]And God called the firmament Heaven. And the evening and the morning were the second day."

From the scripture text we can clearly see God's definition for a day is from evening to evening. Night + Day = one day, then Night + Day = two days.

We know exactly what day Lord Jesus Christ was resurrected for the dead/grave.

The Bible says, "**Matthew 28:1 - 7 [KJV]** [1]In the end of the sabbath, as it began to dawn toward the first *day* of the week, came Mary Magdalene and the other Mary to see the sepulchre. [2]And, behold, there was a great earthquake: for the angel of the Lord descended from heaven, and came and rolled back the stone from the door, and sat upon it. [3]His countenance was like lightning, and his raiment white as snow: [4]And for fear of him the keepers did shake, and became as dead *men*. [5]And the angel answered and said unto the women, Fear not ye: for I know that ye seek Jesus, which was crucified. [6]He is not here: for he is risen, as he said. Come, see the place where the Lord lay. [7]And go quickly, and tell his disciples that he is risen from the dead; and, behold, he goeth before you into Galilee; there shall ye see him: lo, I have told you."

From all of the above information we can easily figure out when Lord Jesus Christ was crucified. All we need to do is count backwards from the first day of the week which is Sunday.

According to God's definition of a day, Sunday starts at Saturday evening. Therefore Saturday evening to Friday evening is one day; Friday evening to Thursday evening is two days; and Thursday evening to Wednesday evening is three days, which means that Lord Jesus Christ was crucified on Good Wednesday!

Lord Jesus Christ makes it very clear that in order for us to worship God it has to include the truth.

The Bible says, "**John 4:19 - 26 [KJV]** [19]The woman saith unto him, Sir, I perceive that thou art a prophet. [20]Our fathers worshipped in this mountain; and ye say, that in Jerusalem is the place where men ought to worship. [21]Jesus saith unto her, Woman, believe me, the hour cometh, when ye shall neither in this mountain, nor yet at Jerusalem, worship the Father. [22]Ye worship ye know not what: we know what we worship: for salvation is of the Jews. [23]But the hour cometh, and now is, when the true worshippers shall worship the Father in spirit and in truth: for the Father seeketh such to worship him. [24]God *is* a Spirit: and they that worship him must worship *him* in spirit and in truth. [25]The woman saith unto him, I know that Messias cometh, which is called Christ: when he is come, he will tell us all things. [26]Jesus saith unto her, I that speak unto thee am *he*."

Notes and Reflection:

Chapter 3: Hard to Interpret Scriptures.

Genesis 6:2 [KJV]
² That the sons of God saw the daughters of men that they *were* fair; and they took them wives of all which they chose.

<u>What does this mean?</u> <u>Did Angels have sex with women on earth</u>?

>———— Scripture Reference: Genesis 6:1-12 ————<

Introduction: The Bible says, "**Hebrews 1:5 [KJV]** ⁵For unto which of the angels said he at any time, Thou art my Son, this day have I begotten thee? And again, I will be to him a Father, and he shall be to me a Son?"

Lord Jesus Christ is the Son of God and every believer in Lord Jesus Christ is also by adoption a son of God.

The Bible says, "**John 1:12 [KJV]** ¹²But as many as received him, to them gave he power to become the sons of God, *even* to them that believe on his name:"

In the Old Testament days, everyone who obeyed and worshiped God was also known as sons of God.

The Bible also says, "**Romans 8:14 [KJV]** ¹⁴For as many as are led by the Spirit of God, they are the sons of God."

Throughout the whole Bible, God refer to mankind as sons of God. The book of <u>**Job**</u> refers to angels as sons of God, but Genesis is talking about mankind as sons of God.

The Bible says, "**Galatians 4:6 [KJV]** ⁶And because ye are sons, God hath sent forth the Spirit of his Son into your hearts, crying, Abba, Father."

The Bible also says, "**1 John 3:1 [KJV]** ¹Behold, what manner of love the Father hath bestowed upon us, that we should be called the sons of God: therefore the world knoweth us not, because it knew him not."

There are many more scriptures in the Bible referring to us/mankind, as sons of God and God as our Father.

<u>The title of this message from God is,</u> *"Lord Jesus Christ had to make mankind acceptable to God; otherwise God would destroy all of mankind the next time."*

The Bible constantly and consistently teaches the total depravity of mankind.

Because Adam the created son of God sinned against God, mankind is a born sinner so corrupt that without intervention in our lives from God, no human being would ever obey and worship God.

In the scripture text God uses His servant Moses to teach us three important facts about the total depravity of mankind.

The first important fact about the total depravity of mankind that God uses His servant Moses to teach us is that, *"Apart from God or spiritually separated from God, mankind will naturally gravitate towards evil"*. Every descendent of Adam is born with an inherited sin nature.

Looking at Genesis chapter 6, verses **1** thru **4**, we see that the scripture text says, "**Genesis 6:1 - 4 [KJV]** ¹And it came to pass, when men began to multiply on the face of the earth, and daughters were born unto them, ²That the sons of God saw the daughters of men that they *were* fair; and they took them wives of all which they chose. ³And the LORD said, My spirit shall not always strive with man, for that he also *is* flesh: yet his days shall be an hundred and twenty years. ⁴There were giants in the earth in those days; and also after that, when the sons of God came in unto the daughters of men, and they bare *children* to them, the same *became* mighty men which *were* of old, men of renown." There is a cycle that mankind goes through continuously, a generation that loves God will have children who drift away from fellowship with God, and their children will drift even further, until there is no one left who cares anything for God. In Genesis chapter five we see that Seth generation was a generation that loved God and called on the name of God. The descendants of Seth drifted away from fellowship with God and married ungodly women, and they produced ungodly children instead of godly children. If this was not true, there would have been more people than just Noah and his family in the Ark.

Illustration: A deacon who was also the president of the young adult choir asked the Pastor, *"why do people follow someone who they know is wrong, instead of the person who is trying to do what's right?"* Without hesitation the Pastor told the deacon that, *"Because people naturally do what's wrong"*.

If we do not faithfully observe spiritual disciplines that keep our minds focused on Lord Jesus Christ, then we will drift out of fellowship with God into apostasy and evil relationships. The scripture text says, "³And the LORD said, My spirit shall not always strive with man, for that he also *is* flesh: yet his days shall be an hundred and twenty years." The New Living Translation of the Bible says, "**Genesis 6:3 [NLT]** ³Then the LORD said, "My Spirit will not put up with humans for such a long time, for they are only mortal flesh. In the future, their normal lifespan will be no more than 120 years."" We know that this has to be a bad interpretation of that verse from/in the New Living Translation of the Bible, because Abraham, Isaac, and Jacob all lived past 120 years of age. Abraham was 175 years old when he died, Isaac was 180 years old when he died, and Israel who is Jacob was a 147 years old when he died. There were other people according to the Bible that were born after the flood and before Abraham who lived from a range of 148 to 438 years old before they died. The true interpretation for that verse is that it took Noah 120 years to build the

Ark. After the Ark was built, loaded up with animals and Noah's family, then <u>God</u> <u>closed</u> the door of the Ark and destroyed everything on land with water that was outside of the Ark. Noah was also used by the Holy Ghost/Spirit to preach to the people during those one hundred and twenty years of building the Ark to repent of their evil deeds, but they did not. The scripture text also says, "'There were giants in the earth in those days; and also after that, when the sons of God came in unto the daughters of men, and they bare *children* to them, the same *became* mighty men which *were* of old, men of renown." God has always had a variety of people. Some of our basketball players could be considered to be giants. There used to be a Championship Wrestler that used to be called the giant because of his height and weight. Giants have always been on the earth, before and after the flood. Goliath was a giant that King David killed. Angels did not have sex with women to make giants before the flood or after the flood. Angels are spirit beings that do not procreate; they do not reproduce like humans do, and human beings do not become Angels when we die! What this means for us is that we need to read and study the whole Bible for ourselves, preferably the King James Version for the most accuracy. We need to know the truth from the Bible, so that we can tell if someone is preaching or teaching the true word of God. There are two primary groups of people on the earth, those who obey and worship God and those who do not obey and do not worship God; those who believe in Lord Jesus Christ and those who do not believe in Lord Jesus Christ. We need to know who we are dealing with in our relationships, is it the naturally corrupt person, who do not obey God and do not worship God or is it the new creature or person in Lord Jesus Christ, who obeys God and worship God?

The next important fact about the total depravity of mankind that God uses His servant Moses to teach us is that, *"Almighty Holy God demands payment for transgressions against His Holy Will"*. Holy God shows mankind His ability to destroy as well as to create.

Looking again at the scripture text, verses **5** thru **7** of the 6th chapter of Genesis say, "**Genesis 6:5 - 7 [KJV]** 5And God saw that the wickedness of man *was* great in the earth, and *that* every imagination of the thoughts of his heart *was* only evil continually. 6And it repented the LORD that he had made man on the earth, and it grieved him at his heart. 7And the LORD said, I will destroy man whom I have created from the face of the earth; both man, and beast, and the creeping thing, and the fowls of the air; for it repenteth me that I have made them." The Bible says, "**Ezekiel 18:4 [KJV]** 4Behold, all souls are mine; as the soul of the father, so also the soul of the son is mine: the soul that sinneth, it shall die."

<u>Illustration:</u> In the United States of America sometimes a good lawyer can get a verdict or sentence from a lower court changed by appealing to a higher court.

There have been human beings throughout the history of mankind who did not worship and obey God, who decided to make up their own laws and purposely refused to recognize the dos and don'ts and authority of God that's found in the Bible. There is no higher court to make an appeal to that can reverse the verdict or sentence of God. Refusing to believe the truth does not make the truth untrue. When a majority of the people or rulers over the people chooses to change what God has commanded mankind to do and not to do, it does not make their changes supersede what God has commanded. Just because a person or people in our society are very rich and/or influential, their

opinions do not supersedes anything that God has commanded mankind to do and not to do. What this means for us is that Almighty Holy God has judged the World before for the disobedience of mankind, and we can count on God to do it again, especially since God has already told us in the Bible, why, when, and how He will once again and permanently deal with disobedient mankind.

Not only does God's servant Moses make known to us that, *"Apart from God or spiritually separated from God, mankind will naturally gravitate towards evil"*, and that, *"Almighty Holy God demands payment for transgressions against His Holy Will"*. His servant Moses also reveals to us that, *"Almighty Holy God shows His love for mankind by preserving Noah's family to repopulate the earth."* Fallen mankind does not have the ability to obey God; without assistance from God.

Looking again for the last time at the scripture text, we see that verses **8** thru **12** of the 6th chapter of Genesis say, "**Genesis 6:8 - 12 [KJV]** **⁸But Noah found grace in the eyes of the LORD. ⁹These *are* the generations of Noah: Noah was a just man *and* perfect in his generations, *and* Noah walked with God.¹⁰And Noah begat three sons, Shem, Ham, and Japheth. ¹¹The earth also was corrupt before God, and the earth was filled with violence. ¹²And God looked upon the earth, and, behold, it was corrupt; for all flesh had corrupted his way upon the earth."** Right before God flooded the whole earth with water to kill all the wicked people off the earth, Holy God showed unearned kindness to eight persons which were Noah and the rest of his family, by rescuing them from the death sentence judgment that God had executed against wicked mankind. Even though the Bible talks about the divine consequences that our disobedient behavior towards God can bring upon us, we can clearly see that it hasn't stopped corrupt mankind from repeating the same mistakes that wicked mankind made during the lifetime of Noah.

Illustration: A middle age man who was serious about sharing the good news of Lord Jesus Christ, was witnessing to one of his supervisors on the job, and he quoted from the Bible, "**Romans 3:23 [KJV]** ²³For all have sinned, and come short of the glory of God;" his supervisor said that he has never sinned, as if he truly believed that, even though most of the employees knew he was corrupt and bragged about having intercourse with women other than his wife.

Unregenerate, unrepentant, wicked mankind does not consider their disobedient behavior towards God as something to be concerned about. What this means for us is that the total depravity of mankind causes him or her to constantly and consistently live a lifestyle that is in rebellion towards God. Fortunately for every one whom God has intervened into our lives, who worship and obey God, will be rescued just like Noah and his family were, from the next destruction and casting of wicked mankind into the eternal burning Lake of Fire!

Conclusion: Now that we fully understand that, *"Lord Jesus Christ had to make mankind acceptable to God; otherwise God would destroy all of mankind the next time,"* and that because Adam the created son of God sinned against God, mankind is a born sinner so corrupt that without intervention in our lives from God, no human being would ever obey and worship God. **What will be our response to this eye opening news about mankind?** Will we finally make up our minds to show our gratitude unto God for intervening in our lives and regenerating our minds, by allowing Lord Jesus Christ to live the Christian life through us?

Will we finally make a conscious decision and commitment in our minds to worship and obey God regardless of what the majority of the people decide to do?

Will we finally make up our minds never to deny the existence of our heavenly Father or Lord Jesus Christ, regardless of what the atheists/evolutionist say?

Notes and Reflection:

Introduction: Most people if not all, who enjoy reading as a hobby will always say that, *"The book is better than the movie"*.

Some people if not all, who enjoy reading the Bible on a daily basis will always say that, *"Reading the Bible yourself, from beginning to end is better than trusting some old traditional sayings about the Bible"*.

There have been too much incorrect teachings about the Bible that has been passed down through the generations that needs to be corrected!

A long time ago, somebody started a false teaching about Ezekiel 28:13-15. They said that Lucifer, now known as Satan the devil worked in the Garden of Eden and was responsible for making it beautiful, but when we read the first and second chapters of the book of Genesis we can clearly see that God says that He did all the work in creating the Heavens and the Earth including the Garden of Eden.

The title of this message from God is, *"Lord Jesus Christ is the only human being who is also God."*

The person who is totally given over to the devil will compete against God for glory.

In the scripture text God uses the Prophet Ezekiel to teach us three important facts about a person possessed by Satan the devil.

The first important fact about a person possessed by the devil that God uses the Prophet Ezekiel to teach us is that, *"Satan the devil believes himself to be smart and powerful enough to replace Almighty Holy God"*. The devil is able to use many human beings against God and the people of God.

> Looking at Ezekiel chapter 28, verses **1** thru **10**, we see that the scripture text says, "**Ezekiel 28:1 - 10 [KJV]** ¹The word of the LORD came again unto me, saying, ²Son of man, say unto the prince of Tyrus, Thus saith the Lord GOD; Because thine heart *is* lifted up, and thou hast said, I *am* a God, I sit *in* the seat of God, in the midst of the seas; yet thou *art* a man, and not God, though thou set thine heart as the heart of God: ³Behold, thou *art* wiser than Daniel; there is no secret that they can hide from thee: ⁴With thy wisdom and with thine understanding thou hast gotten thee riches, and hast gotten gold and silver into thy treasures: ⁵By thy great wisdom *and* by thy traffic hast thou increased thy riches, and thine heart is lifted up because of thy riches: ⁶Therefore thus saith the Lord GOD; Because thou hast set thine heart as the heart of God; ⁷Behold, therefore I will bring strangers upon thee, the terrible of the nations: and they shall draw their swords against the beauty of thy wisdom, and they shall defile thy brightness. ⁸They shall bring thee down to the pit, and thou shalt die the deaths of *them that are* slain in the midst of the seas. ⁹Wilt thou yet say before him that slayeth thee, I *am* God? but thou *shalt be* a man, and no God, in the hand of him that

slayeth thee. ¹⁰Thou shalt die the deaths of the uncircumcised by the hand of strangers: for I have spoken *it*, saith the Lord GOD." A person that will rebel against God and His authority, will rebel against parents and everybody else authority. The scripture text says, "⁶Therefore thus saith the Lord GOD; Because thou hast set thine heart as the heart of God; ⁷Behold, therefore I will bring strangers upon thee, the terrible of the nations: and they shall draw their swords against the beauty of thy wisdom, and they shall defile thy brightness." **Lord GOD** means Adonai Jehovah or the master of our service and redeemer. God used the Prophet Ezekiel to deliver this message to the prince of Tyrus, a man who was being used and controlled by Satan the devil. Satan the devil had made this person his puppet to do whatever the devil desired. The prince of Tyrus was so completely possessed by the devil that his character and existence was the same as that of the devil.

Illustration: Scientists say that they have cloned animals and they are thinking about cloning human beings. One of the concerns or questions that they have discussed is whether or not the cloned human will think exactly like the original human.

A demon or devil possessed person will think and do whatever the devil or demon commands them to do. God is speaking to both the human being and the devil who is occupying the body of the human being. The wisdom that this prince had that made him rich came directly from the devil. What this means for us is that we can recognize a demon or devil possessed person by their evil character, prideful boasting of any achievement, endless pursuit of fame and glory; total disrespect for Almighty Holy God, with an abnormal thirst for power. A believer cannot be possessed by a demon or the devil, because he or she is indwelt by God the Holy Ghost. The Bible says, "**1 John 4:4 [KJV]** ⁴Ye are of God, little children, and have overcome them: because greater is he that is in you, than he that is in the world."

The next important fact about a person possessed by the devil that God uses the Prophet Ezekiel to teach us is that, *"Transgressions against God cause His creation to lose its special beauty"*. Every creature or person is created with a special beauty by God.

Looking again at the scripture text, verses **11** thru **16** of the 28ᵗʰ chapter of Ezekiel say, "**Ezekiel 28:11 - 16 [KJV]** ¹¹Moreover the word of the LORD came unto me, saying, ¹²Son of man, take up a lamentation upon the king of Tyrus, and say unto him, Thus saith the Lord GOD; Thou sealest up the sum, full of wisdom, and perfect in beauty. ¹³Thou hast been in Eden the garden of God; every precious stone *was* thy covering, the sardius, topaz, and the diamond, the beryl, the onyx, and the jasper, the sapphire, the emerald, and the carbuncle, and gold: the workmanship of thy tabrets and of thy pipes was prepared in thee in the day that thou wast created. ¹⁴Thou *art* the anointed cherub that covereth; and I have set thee *so*: thou wast upon the holy mountain of God; thou hast walked up and down in the midst of the stones of fire. ¹⁵Thou *wast* perfect in thy ways from the day that thou wast created, till iniquity was found in thee. ¹⁶By the multitude of thy merchandise they have filled the midst of thee with violence, and thou hast sinned: therefore I will cast thee as profane out of the mountain of God: and I will destroy thee, O covering cherub, from the midst of the stones of fire." The scripture text is speaking directly to the evil spirit known as Satan the devil who has taken control of this person's body and mind.

<u>Illustration:</u> A man fell deeply in love with a beautiful and talented woman and enjoyed the feeling of being in love with her, but over the course of ten years her mean behavior towards him caused his love for her to fade away.

God created Lucifer as the most beautiful, talented, and powerful of the angels. Lucifer was also given great wisdom above the other angels. Lucifer had access to all of God's creation, even the Garden of Eden where he used Adam's wife to cause Adam to sin against God and condemn mankind to spiritual separation from Almighty Holy God. The scripture text says, "every precious stone *was* thy covering, the sardius, topaz, and the diamond, the beryl, the onyx, and the jasper, the sapphire, the emerald, and the carbuncle, and gold:" This is not a reference to Lucifer beautifying the Garden of Eden or Earth. The Bible says this about the identity of God the Father, "**Revelation 4:3 [KJV]** [3] And he that sat was to look upon like a jasper and a sardine stone: and *there was* a rainbow round about the throne, in sight like unto an emerald." Spirit beings are identified by brightness and colors of light that they emit. The precious stones and color gold used to describe Lucifer, give us a very clear picture of how beautiful this angel was. After causing mankind through Adam to sin/rebel against God and a third of the angels to also rebel against God, Lucifer has been stripped of his beauty and his name changed to Satan the devil. Satan and his demons (*the fallen angels*) are on the earth constantly tempting mankind to sin against God because they hate God and mankind. What this means for us is that if we choose to follow Satan the devil instead of Lord Jesus Christ, then we will be set aside like Satan and his demons for final destruction, which is eternal torment in the Lake of Fire forever.

Not only does the Prophet Ezekiel make known to us that, *"Satan the devil believes himself to be smart and powerful enough to replace Almighty Holy God"*, and that, *"Transgressions against God cause His creation to lose its special beauty"*. The Prophet Ezekiel also reveals to us that, *"Continual rebellion and sinning against God causes a person to have a reprobate mind."* God will not permit a reprobate mind to exist/live in His permanent Kingdom.

Looking again for the last time at the scripture text, we see that verses **17** thru **19** of the 28th chapter of Ezekiel say, "**Ezekiel 28:17 - 19 [KJV]** [17]Thine heart was lifted up because of thy beauty, thou hast corrupted thy wisdom by reason of thy brightness: I will cast thee to the ground, I will lay thee before kings, that they may behold thee. [18]Thou hast defiled thy sanctuaries by the multitude of thine iniquities, by the iniquity of thy traffic; therefore will I bring forth a fire from the midst of thee, it shall devour thee, and I will bring thee to ashes upon the earth in the sight of all them that behold thee. [19]All they that know thee among the people shall be astonished at thee: thou shalt be a terror, and never *shalt* thou *be* any more." The final destiny of mankind is one of two places, the **Lake of Fire** or in **Heaven** with God. The prince of Tyrus was totally and completely possessed by the devil; therefore God terminated his existence on earth, because he had given himself to serving the evil desires of the devil! Once a person becomes the servant of the devil, he or she will never adhere to or acknowledge the authority of God; they are given over to a reprobate mind!

<u>Illustration:</u> A person is labeled a serial killer when he or she has developed a lifestyle of murdering unsuspecting people. If apprehended, a serial killer is removed from society and placed in jail or a mental institution. A serial killer will not knowingly by the government be allowed to live among other people, because they are a danger to other people.

What this means for us is that thinking and living our lives under the influence of Satan the devil is the path to destruction, because anyone who choose that path will receive divine and everlasting consequences from Almighty Holy God.

Conclusion: Now that we fully understand that, *"Lord Jesus Christ is the only human being who is also God,"* and that the person who is totally given over to the devil will compete against God for glory.

<u>What will we do when we are tempted to become a follower of the devil</u>?

If we haven't already done so, will we accept Lord Jesus Christ as our Savior and make Him our master, so that we do not embrace the character of Satan the devil and become an evil and prideful person?

If we haven't already done so, will we accept Lord Jesus Christ as our Savior and make Him our master, so that we do not become a permanent child of the devil, behaving in a wicked and evil manner like so many others who hate Lord Jesus Christ?

If we haven't already done so, will we accept Lord Jesus Christ as our Savior and make Him our master, so that we do not end up in the Lake of fire which is the final and permanent destination for everyone with a reprobate mind?

Notes and Reflection:

Matthew 5:39 [KJV]

[39] But I say unto you, That ye resist not evil: but whosoever shall smite thee on thy right cheek, turn to him the other also.

What does this mean? Do we suppose to not defend ourselves and let somebody beat us to death?

>—— Scripture Reference: Matthew 5:38-42 ——<

Introduction: As we continue to grow in grace and the knowledge of our Lord and Savior Jesus Christ, we can see that Lord Jesus Christ wants us to depend on Him, instead of depending on ourselves or any other person.

We also understand that Lord Jesus Christ is everything there is; there is nothing without Lord Jesus Christ.

Lord Jesus Christ is life, rest, peace, and joy. We can truly put all our trust and faith in Lord Jesus Christ and never fear being disappointed.

The title of this message from God is, *"Lord Jesus Christ will punish evildoers who mistreat believers."*

The Bible says, "**Romans 12:17 - 21 [KJV]** [17]Recompense to no man evil for evil. Provide things honest in the sight of all men. [18]If it be possible, as much as lieth in you, live peaceably with all men. [19]Dearly beloved, avenge not yourselves, but *rather* give place unto wrath: for it is written, Vengeance *is* mine; I will repay, saith the Lord. [20]Therefore if thine enemy hunger, feed him; if he thirst, give him drink: for in so doing thou shalt heap coals of fire on his head. [21]Be not overcome of evil, but overcome evil with good."

In the scripture text our Lord gives us three examples of godly responses to an evildoer's evil behavior.

The first godly response to an evildoer's evil behavior that our Lord gives us is that, *"Lord Jesus Christ commands us to refrain from the use of physical violence"*. Love does not cause physical pain to another person.

Looking at Matthew chapter 5, verses **38** and **39**, we see that the scripture text says, "**Matthew 5:38 - 39 [KJV]** ³⁸Ye have heard that it hath been said, An eye for an eye, and a tooth for a tooth: ³⁹But I say unto you, That ye resist not evil: but whosoever shall smite thee on thy right cheek, turn to him the other also.**" In the scripture text we can clearly see the difference in the Mosaic Law system compared to the Kingdom of Heaven system. According to the Law, if a person did bodily harm to another person, then that person should receive the same bodily harm in return. In the Kingdom of Heaven where Lord Jesus Christ is King we are commanded to always return love whenever we are mistreated, knowing that Lord Jesus Christ will make sure that justice is served on our behalf.

Illustration: A man who was convicted of rape and murder as well as attempted rape, case came up for parole and there was some saying that he was eligible for parole and they were considering the possibility of letting him out of jail, back into the community that he had terrorized.

If we worry about making sure justice is properly served equally among all people, then we will never get around to doing what Lord Jesus Christ has commanded us to do concerning the Great Commission of spreading the gospel of Lord Jesus Christ throughout the World. We have to let Lord Jesus Christ choose for us the battles of injustice that He would have us to fight against, and refrain from choosing according to our will or somebody else's will, our battles to fight. What this means for us is that non-violence is a powerful weapon that we can use. Non-violence has a way of exposing the evil deeds of evildoers not only to everybody else, but also to the evildoers. Retaliation gives evildoers the justification they desire to continue to be evil.

The next godly response to an evildoer's evil behavior that our Lord gives us is that, *"Lord Jesus Christ commands us to refrain from verbal disputes"*. Love does not choose to argue with another person.

Looking again at the scripture text, verse **40** of the 5ᵗʰ chapter of Matthew say, "**Matthew 5:40 [KJV]** ⁴⁰And if any man will sue thee at the law, and take away thy coat, let him have *thy* cloak also.**" There are a multitude of lawsuits being tried continuously in the United States of America; so many people are using the Judicial Courts System to have their selfish demands granted.

Illustration: The most common legal dispute is that of a successful movie actress who decided to have a baby from her boyfriend whom she's not married to. For whatever reason they disagreed about something and decided that their relationship is over, then they start to argue about the custody and visitation rights concerning the out of wedlock child.

As followers of Lord Jesus Christ we should try to avoid getting involved in long drawn out court cases if at all possible. Lord Jesus Christ is our judge and jury, if a court case is going to cost us more than what a person is suing us for, then the smart thing to do would be to let them have what they want. We do not need to waste a lot of money and time to prove that we can win. What this means for us is that there are court cases that Lord Jesus Christ will choose for us to fight, but until then we should do everything within our power to stay out of the Judicial Courts System, especially when it involves another believer.

Not only does the scripture text make known to us that, *"Lord Jesus Christ commands us to refrain from the use of physical violence"*, and that, *"Lord Jesus Christ commands us to refrain from verbal disputes"*. The scripture text also reveals to us that, *"Lord Jesus Christ commands us to help those who are in need of our assistance."* Love is eager to help another person in need.

Looking again for the last time at the scripture text, we see that verses **41** thru **42** of the 5th chapter of Matthew say, "**Matthew 5:41 - 42 (KJV)** **41**And whosoever shall compel thee to go a mile, go with him twain. **42**Give to him that asketh thee, and from him that would borrow of thee turn not thou away."

Illustration: A deacon of a local church was teaching Bible study class one summer day when a homeless guy came in the church and asked for five dollars to get some mosquito spray, because he was sleeping by the railroad tracks at night. The deacon thought for a moment that he might buy liquor with the money, but felt the Holy Ghost/Spirit urging him to give him the money, so he gave him the five dollars. Several years later the deacon was buying food from a supermarket near the church that he attends, and a man walked up to him and hugged him real tight in the store in front of everybody, to the deacon's surprise when the man let him go, stepped back and said, *"Thank you,"* the deacon recognized who the man was. It was the homeless guy, but he had a haircut and clean clothing on him and money to spend. God had blessed that homeless guy and cleaned him up.

We do not know or understand how God works in other people lives, our duty is to be obedient with the resources that God has entrusted us with. What this means for us is that whenever God urges us to help someone who is in need, whether it be somebody we know or a stranger, our responsibility is to obey and allow God to use us to help that individual or individuals.

Conclusion: Now that we fully understand that, *"Lord Jesus Christ will punish evildoers who mistreat believers,"* and that Lord Jesus Christ says, "Vengeance *is* mine; I will repay".

How will these commandments of Lord Jesus Christ affect our behavior as followers of Lord Jesus Christ?

Will we do our best to be non-violent in obedience to Lord Jesus Christ?

Will we do our best to stay out of arguments in obedience to Lord Jesus Christ?

Will we do our best to help those who are in need of our help, especially those of the household of faith in obedience to Lord Jesus Christ?

Notes and Reflection:

Matthew 6:13 [KJV] ¹³And lead us not into temptation, but deliver us from evil: For thine is the kingdom, and the power, and the glory, for ever. Amen.

What exactly does this mean because the Bible says, "**James 1:13 [KJV]** ¹³Let no man say when he is tempted, I am tempted of God: for God cannot be tempted with evil, neither tempteth he any man:"

The Disciples Prayer

⤐—— Scripture Reference: Matthew 6:9-13 ——⤎

Introduction: Matthew 6:9 and Luke 11:2 are the start of what is traditionally known as the Lord's Prayer, but if the truth be told, they should be referred to as the Disciples Prayer. This is the prayer that Lord Jesus Christ gave His followers to pray. Please read below from both places that this prayer is found in the Bible.

Luke 11:1 - 4 [KJV] ¹And it came to pass, that, as he was praying in a certain place, when he ceased, one of his disciples said unto him, Lord, teach us to pray, as John also taught his disciples. ²And he said unto them, When ye pray, say, Our Father which art in heaven, Hallowed be thy name. Thy kingdom come. Thy will be done, as in heaven, so in earth.³Give us day by day our daily bread. ⁴And forgive us our sins; for we also forgive every one that is indebted to us. And lead us not into temptation; but deliver us from evil.

Matthew 6:9 - 13 [KJV] ⁹After this manner therefore pray ye: Our Father which art in heaven, Hallowed be thy name.¹⁰Thy kingdom come. Thy will be done in earth, as *it is* in heaven.¹¹Give us this day our daily bread. ¹²And forgive us our debts, as we forgive our debtors. ¹³And lead us not into temptation, but deliver us from evil: For thine is the kingdom, and the power, and the glory, for ever. Amen.

A very important observation to note in this prayer is the omission of the words "*I*" and "*me*" or "*my*"; and the inclusion of the words "*our*", "*us*" and "*we*".

According to this prayer we are supposed to pray as a body of believers instead of an individual.

This is a prayer that many believers feel inspired to pray at least once every day.

It is a perfect prayer that God will answer; we know that to be true because it came from God in the person of Lord Jesus Christ.

This prayer also serves as a model for any other prayer requests that we make unto God.

The title of this message from God is, "*Lord Jesus Christ gives His followers the perfect prayer to pray unto God.*"

We communicate with God our Creator and develop our relationship with God through prayer.

In the scripture text Lord Jesus Christ give us three important requests that we should make when we pray.

The first important request that we should make when we pray is, *"As followers of Lord Jesus Christ we should pray for the Holy Will of God to be done"*. Nothing good or bad happens unless God allows it.

Looking at Matthew chapter 6, verses **9** and **10**, we see that the scripture text says, "**Matthew 6:9 - 10 [KJV]** ⁹**After this manner therefore pray ye: Our Father which art in heaven, Hallowed be thy name. ¹⁰Thy kingdom come. Thy will be done in earth, as *it is* in heaven.**" Answered prayer is prayer that is prayed according to God's Will, instead of our selfish will. There should be a certain amount of holy reverence for God when we are praying unto God. This prayer lets us know clearly what God desires for us to ask Him for, and how we should approach God when we ask.

Illustration: A man and a woman wanted to get intimate with each other, but they did not want to do it out of wedlock; therefore they decided to get married within a short period of time before they got to know each other.

We get to know God better whenever we pray unto God on a regular basis. What this means for us is that because God is sovereign, the only prayers that He will answer are those according to what He has decided to accomplish in and for mankind.

The next important request that we should make when we pray is, *"As followers of Lord Jesus Christ we should pray for our daily necessities"*. There are some things that believers need on a daily basis.

Looking again at the scripture text, verses **11** and **12** of the 6ᵗʰ chapter of Matthew say, "**Matthew 6:11 - 12 [KJV]** ¹¹**Give us this day our daily bread. ¹²And forgive us our debts, as we forgive our debtors.**" Food is needed for our bodies to function properly and stay healthy. Forgiveness from God is needed in order for us to have fellowship with God on a daily basis. Being saved does not keep us from making mistakes and sinning against God. Hopefully whatever sin we commit against God is one that is done through ignorance.

Illustration: A Christian man wrote a letter to an ex-girlfriend and asked her to forgive him of the hurt that he had caused her in the past. She read the letter and they started communicating again on a very friendly basis, but she never said I forgive you to the man.

The Bible says, "**1 John 1:9 [KJV]** ⁹**If we confess our sins, he is faithful and just to forgive us *our* sins, and to cleanse us from all unrighteousness.**" What this means for us is that there are times in our lives when we have sinned against God without knowing that we were doing something wrong, but when we realized that we had or were sinning, then we repented and turned away from that particular sin. Whenever we sincerely ask God for His forgiveness, God forgives us.

Not only does Lord Jesus Christ make known to us that, *"As followers of Lord Jesus Christ we should pray for the Holy Will of God to be done"*, and that, *"As followers of Lord Jesus Christ we should pray for our daily necessities"*. Lord Jesus Christ also reveals to us that, *"As followers of Lord Jesus Christ we should pray for God's hedge of protection around us."* Evildoers are relentless in their pursuit to destroy the righteous.

Looking again for the last time at the scripture text, we see that verse **13** of the 6th chapter of Matthew says, "**Matthew 6:13 [KJV]** 13**And lead us not into temptation, but deliver us from evil: For thine is the kingdom, and the power, and the glory, for ever. Amen.**"

<u>Illustration:</u> The Old Testament gives a good example of the kind of temptation or testing that this prayer precludes when we consider the life of Job and how God allowed the Devil to do some wicked things to him. Job lost everything that he owned and everybody that he loved except his wife, and she was an unreasonable complainer.

Whenever we read or hear the daily news, we always read and hear something bad or wicked about people who are doing something evil to themselves or somebody else. When we pray this prayer, we are asking God to keep His hedge of protection around us; so that the devil or demons will not be able to cause us to do something wicked to ourselves or anybody else. The Bible says, "**Job 1:9 - 11 [KJV]** 9**Then Satan answered the LORD, and said, Doth Job fear God for nought?** 10**Hast not thou made an hedge about him, and about his house, and about all that he hath on every side? thou hast blessed the work of his hands, and his substance is increased in the land.** 11**But put forth thine hand now, and touch all that he hath, and he will curse thee to thy face.**" What this means for us is that because of the sovereignty of God, nothing in creation can happen unless God allows it. We need to pray that God does not allow Satan the devil or any demons to put us to the test. We know that God will keep us through the test, but by no means will it be a pleasant experience.

Conclusion: Now that we know that, *"Lord Jesus Christ gives His followers the perfect prayer to pray unto God,"* and that we communicate with God our Creator and develop our relationship with God through prayer.

<u>What will we do in order for this to happen and continue to happen in our life on a continuous daily basis?</u>

Will we make a habit of praying for God's Holy Will to be done every day when we pray?

Will we make a habit of praying for the daily necessities that we need every day when we pray?

Will we make a habit of praying for God's hedge of protection around us, for our protection from the evil one, every day when we pray?

Please note that when we pray we should pray for all believers, not just ourselves only!

Notes and Reflection:

Matthew 11:12 [KJV] ¹²And from the days of John the Baptist until now the kingdom of heaven suffereth violence, and the violent take it by force.

<u>What does this mean?</u> <u>How does the kingdom of heaven suffers violence?</u>

⤳—— <u>Scripture Reference: Matthew 11:1-15</u> ——⤶

Introduction: The four accounts of the gospel, Matthew, Mark, Luke, and John all preach and teach the good news of Lord Jesus Christ from a different perspective.

The gospel account according to **John** places the emphasis on the deity of Lord Jesus Christ.

The gospel account according to **Luke** focuses on the humanity of Lord Jesus Christ.

The gospel account according to **Mark** reveals Lord Jesus Christ as the obedient servant.

The gospel account according to **Matthew** declares the kingship of Lord Jesus Christ as the rightful heir to the throne of King David.

<u>The title of this message from God is,</u> *"Lord Jesus Christ is the Kingdom of Heaven."*

In the same manner that Lord Jesus Christ is the head of the church body of Christ or Church, Lord Jesus Christ is also the King of the Kingdom of Heaven.

<u>In the scripture text God uses the Apostle Matthew to show us three important reasons to believe that Lord Jesus Christ is the Messiah.</u>

The first important reason for believing Lord Jesus Christ to be the Messiah, that God uses the Apostle Matthew to show us is that, *"Lord Jesus Christ has the credentials of the Messiah"*. Old Testament prophets predicted what the Messiah would do when He come to His people.

Looking at Matthew chapter 11, verses **1** thru **6**, we see that the scripture text says, "**Matthew 11:1 - 6 [KJV]** ¹And it came to pass, when Jesus had made an end of commanding his twelve disciples, he departed thence to teach and to preach in their cities. ²Now when John had heard in the prison the works of Christ, he sent two of his disciples, ³And said unto him, Art thou he that should come, or do we look for another? ⁴Jesus answered and said unto them, Go and show John again those things which ye do hear and see: ⁵The blind receive their sight, and the lame walk, the lepers are cleansed, and the deaf hear, the dead are raised up, and the poor have the gospel preached to them. ⁶And blessed is *he*, whosoever shall not be offended in me." The nation of Israel was well aware of the things that the predicted Messiah would do when He comes. Lord Jesus Christ is the only human being that can say, *"Let my works speak for ME"* and be justified.

<u>Illustration:</u>   A man started his own business as a handyman, because he got tired of working hard and his boss was the only one getting rich. The man started out with one job at a time, and did very good work. His work was so good that his clients started recommending him to their friends and his business grew to the point that he had to hire other workers to accommodate all his customers.

A successful business starts with a good reputation, and a good reputation comes from good reliable work habits. Everything that Lord Jesus Christ did for people were all considered to be good deeds, the exact kind of good deeds that only the Messiah was predicted to do and only the Messiah could do, when He comes. What this means for us is that Lord Jesus Christ good works not only speaks for Himself, but they also speaks for us as well. After receiving salvation through Lord Jesus Christ, we are left on the earth in His employ to be used by Lord Jesus Christ, to continue the good work that He has started in the World.

The next important reason for believing Lord Jesus Christ to be the Messiah, that God uses the Apostle Matthew to show us is that, *"John the Baptist introduced the Messiah to the nation of Israel"*. John the Baptist came in the spirit of the Old Testament prophet Elijah.

Looking again at the scripture text, verses **7** thru **11** of the 11ᵗʰ chapter of Matthew say, "**Matthew 11:7 - 11 [KJV]** ⁷**And as they departed, Jesus began to say unto the multitudes concerning John, What went ye out into the wilderness to see? A reed shaken with the wind? ⁸But what went ye out for to see? A man clothed in soft raiment? behold, they that wear soft *clothing* are in kings' houses. ⁹But what went ye out for to see? A prophet? yea, I say unto you, and more than a prophet. ¹⁰For this is *he*, of whom it is written, Behold, I send my messenger before thy face, which shall prepare thy way before thee. ¹¹Verily I say unto you, Among them that are born of women there hath not risen a greater than John the Baptist: notwithstanding he that is least in the kingdom of heaven is greater than he.**" Lord Jesus Christ describes John the Baptist as a great prophet sent into the World with the special assignment of preparing the minds or hearts of the people of the nation of Israel to receive the Messiah at His coming.

<u>Illustration:</u> Most Masters of Ceremony are gifted at making even the most ordinary person seem important.

Lord Jesus Christ said that John the Baptist was the greatest person ever born of a woman because he was granted the greatest privilege that any human being has been given by introducing/ identifying the Messiah to the World. Lord Jesus Christ lets us know that being a member of His kingdom, the Kingdom of Heaven is greater than the greatest accomplishment that any human being can make on the earth. Lord Jesus Christ says, "**Matthew 6:33 [KJV]** ³³ But seek ye first the kingdom of God, and his righteousness; and all these things shall be added unto you." What this means for us is that the obedience of John the Baptist in introducing Jesus the Messiah to the nation of Israel also impacted mankind throughout the whole earth. Not only does the nation of Israel benefits from the coming of Lord Jesus Christ into His creation, the other nations of the earth benefits as well.

Not only does the Apostle Matthew make known to us that, *"Lord Jesus Christ has the credentials of the Messiah"*, and that, *"John the Baptist introduced the Messiah to the nation of Israel"*. The Apostle Matthew also reveals to us that, *"Lord Jesus Christ reveals His suffering as the infinite God-Man."* From the day of His incarnation thru His death on the cross Lord Jesus Christ suffered violence.

Looking again for the last time at the scripture text, we see that verses **12** thru **15** of the 11th chapter of Matthew says, "**Matthew 11:12 - 15 [KJV]** 12And from the days of John the Baptist until now the kingdom of heaven suffereth violence, and the violent take it by force. 13For all the prophets and the law prophesied until John. 14And if ye will receive *it*, this is Elias, which was for to come. 15He that hath ears to hear, let him hear."

<u>Illustration:</u> Rock concerts are paid for in advance by the fans that purchase the tickets months before the actual performance takes place. An announcement of a concert is made and the fans will purchase their tickets months before the band and/or singer actually appear.

Old Testament prophets predicted that the Messiah would come, but they never lived to see it happen. John the Baptist is the prophet who not only lived to see the arrival of the Messiah; he also introduced Him to the World. What this means for us is that Lord Jesus Christ *(The Messiah)* had a murder attempt upon His life as a child, and for three years once He started His ministry on the earth there were attempts and plans to murder Him. Finally at the end of His three years of ministry on the earth violent/evil/wicked men were allowed to crucify Lord Jesus Christ. Lord Jesus Christ is the Kingdom of Heaven that suffered violence.

Conclusion: Now that we fully understand that, *"Lord Jesus Christ is the Kingdom of Heaven,"* and that in the same manner that Lord Jesus Christ is the head of the church body of Christ or Church, Lord Jesus Christ is also the King of the Kingdom of Heaven.

<u>How will this valuable information open our mind to see Lord Jesus Christ more clearly?</u>

Do we know that the only thing we can say towards our salvation is, *"Let the finished work of Lord Jesus Christ on the cross speak for me"*?

Do we understand that just like John the Baptist, the best thing that we can possible do during our life time, is be a witness unto Lord Jesus Christ?

Do we clearly see that Lord Jesus Christ time on earth was full of hatred and violence towards Him in the first century and also today?

Notes and Reflection:

Luke 16:8 [KJV] ⁸And the lord commended the unjust steward, because he had done wisely: for the children of this world are in their generation wiser than the children of light.

<u>What does this mean</u>? <u>Why is the unjust steward being commended instead of reprimanded?</u>

Scripture Reference: Luke 16:1-13

Introduction: The constant begging of local churches and other Christian organizations for money is a bad witness unto Lord Jesus Christ.

Many believers and unbelievers are turned off from going to Church services, because there's more emphasis placed on fundraising than on Lord Jesus Christ.

It's wrong for any church leader to make the members believe that giving money to the local church is a prerequisite to being accepted into Heaven.

Whenever the messages during most local church services always end with an emphasis on the congregation giving of money to the local church, then we have to wonder if that local church leadership is worshipping God or the dollar bill.

Lord Jesus Christ is more than able and willing to provide for His Church. If local church leadership would simply be obedient unto Lord Jesus Christ, they would not have any financial problems to worry about.

The title of this message from God is, *"Every believer should be a good steward unto Lord Jesus Christ."*

As followers of Lord Jesus Christ, we need to let Lord Jesus Christ by way of the Holy Ghost/Spirit, instruct us on how and where to spend the money and use the resources that God has given us.

In the scripture text Lord Jesus Christ uses a story to illustrate three important components of good stewardship.

The first important component of good stewardship that Lord Jesus Christ illustrates in a story is that, *"Lord Jesus Christ wants His followers to have a financial plan"*. Every believer should have a comprehensive strategy for monies and resources.

Looking at Luke chapter 16, verses **1** thru **9**, we see that the scripture text says, "**Luke 16:1 - 9 [KJV]** **¹And he said also unto his disciples, There was a certain rich man, which had a steward; and the same was accused unto him that he had wasted his goods. ²And he called him, and said unto him, How is it that I hear this of thee? give an account of thy stewardship; for thou mayest be no longer steward. ³Then the steward said within himself, What shall I do? for my lord taketh away from me the stewardship: I cannot dig; to beg I am ashamed. ⁴I am resolved what to do, that, when I am put out of the stewardship, they may receive me into their houses. ⁵So he called every one of his lord's debtors *unto him*, and said unto the first, How much owest thou unto my lord? ⁶And he said, An hundred measures of oil. And he said unto him, Take thy bill, and sit down quickly, and write fifty. ⁷Then said he to another, And how much owest thou? And he said, An hundred measures of wheat. And he said unto him, Take thy bill, and write fourscore. ⁸And the lord commended the unjust steward, because he had done wisely: for the children of this world are in their generation wiser than the children of light. ⁹And I say unto you, Make to yourselves friends of the mammon of unrighteousness; that, when ye fail, they may receive you into everlasting habitations.**" In the scripture text we see a person making detailed preparations for the future after being told that he will be unemployed by his employer. Notice how the man considers what he is _un_able to do and what he is able to do; therefore the man was wise enough to use whatever status and influence that he still had, to prepare the best future for himself that he possibly can. The scripture text says, "**⁹And I say unto you, Make to yourselves friends of the mammon of unrighteousness; that, when ye fail, they may receive you into everlasting habitations.**" Lord Jesus Christ is saying that if we use the monies and resources that He has allocated to us for His purposes on earth, then we will be storing up treasures in Heaven; we will be rewarded in Heaven for our good stewardship on the earth. Many of us who say that we are Christians (*followers of Lord Jesus Christ*) do not make any preparations for the future with the resources and monies that God has allocated to us.

<u>Illustration:</u> Two young men who grew up playing basketball together in school considered themselves to be friends, but after graduating from high school, one of them went on to college and the other did not. The one who went to college came back to his hometown with a college degree and was able to get a good paying job/career that paid him a lot of money. The one who did not go to college ended up with a very hard low paying job and became bitter towards his friend that went to college. The two men stopped being friends simply because one made better preparations for the future than the other.

What this means for us is that we have a responsibility unto Lord Jesus Christ to use the monies and resources that He has allocated to us to the best of our ability, which means that we need to have a spending plan that includes receiving instructions from Lord Jesus Christ by way of the Holy Ghost/Spirit on how to use the monies and resources which He has entrusted us with. We are not at liberty to waste money and resources on selfish creature pleasures for ourselves.

The next important component of good stewardship that Lord Jesus Christ illustrates in a story is that, *"Every believer should faithfully give to the ministry of Lord Jesus Christ in some capacity"*. True followers of Lord Jesus Christ will use their resources to glorify God.

Looking again at the scripture text, verses **10** thru **12** of the 16th chapter of Luke say, "**Luke 16:10 - 12 [KJV]** ¹⁰He that is faithful in that which is least is faithful also in much: and he that is unjust in the least is unjust also in much. ¹¹If therefore ye have not been faithful in the unrighteous mammon, who will commit to your trust the true *riches*? ¹²And if ye have not been faithful in that which is another man's, who shall give you that which is your own?" God's ultimate goal for mankind is Christ-like character. The sanctification process that God puts believers through consists of trials or tests to build our character and also to show us where we are still coming up short in our spiritual maturity. If we continue to get angry about every little thing or continue to take/steal small items from our employer, then we are not allowing Lord Jesus Christ by way of the Holy Ghost to live the Christian life through us.

Illustration: A local church member started noticing that a very influential deacon who didn't attend church on a regular basis would always show up for the big church fundraisers like the church anniversary etc. That church member found out that the deacon would always end up in the finance room where he would get a secret amount of the money from the fundraiser for himself.

To be a good witness unto Lord Jesus Christ we have to be under the control of Lord Jesus Christ by way of God the Holy Ghost. If we continue to be selfish, constantly demanding our so-called rights, then we will never have the teachable spirit in us that's needed to learn from God. What this means for us is that, we should be giving to ministry in some capacity, not takers, and if we are not trustworthy with the property of our employer or associates, then we are not ready for God to trust us with spiritual truths and spiritual blessings, because we continue to depend on ourselves instead of Lord Jesus Christ.

Not only does Lord Jesus Christ make known to us that, *"Lord Jesus Christ wants His followers to have a financial plan"*, and that, *"Every believer should faithfully give to the ministry of Lord Jesus Christ in some capacity"*. Lord Jesus Christ also reveals to us that, *"Every believer should be a loyal and faithful servant unto Lord Jesus Christ."* Lord Jesus Christ wants us to be dependable servants.

Looking again for the last time at the scripture text, we see that verse **13** of the 16th chapter of Luke says, "**Luke 16:13 (KJV)** ¹³No servant can serve two masters: for either he will hate the one, and love the other; or else he will hold to the one, and despise the other. Ye cannot serve God and mammon."

Illustration: A deacon told his newly wed wife a year after the wedding when God called him to be a Pastor, *"You are going to be a preacher's wife,"* and she said, *"God didn't say anything to me about it"*. Needless to say, one of her reasons for divorcing him when times got bad was that he was doing too much ministry and things didn't look like they were going to change.

The old saying is true, *"You can't have your cake and eat it too".* It's either or, not both. The riches and material things/wealth of the evil world system that we live in are in opposition to God and the things of God. Many individuals who have accumulated millions and billions of dollars put their faith and trust in their money instead of Lord Jesus Christ. The Bible says, **"Matthew 6:33 [KJV]** [33] But seek ye first the kingdom of God, and his righteousness; and all these things shall be added unto you." What this means for us is that, it is impossible for us to be totally committed to serving Lord Jesus Christ if we are also trying to earn all the money and riches in the World. The local churches should depend on Lord Jesus Christ instead of people. Church leaders should always look to Lord Jesus Christ for their financial needs to be met.

Conclusion: Now that we fully understand that, *"Every believer should be a good steward unto Lord Jesus Christ,"* and that as followers of Lord Jesus Christ, we need to let Lord Jesus Christ by way of the Holy Ghost/Spirit, instruct us on how and where to spend the money and use the resources that God has given us.

What will we do to become a good steward?

Will we start allowing Lord Jesus Christ by way of the Holy Ghost to dictate to us how to spend His money that He has entrusted us with?

Will we stop living independent of Lord Jesus Christ?

Will we stop trying to put our faith in money and God?

Notes and Reflection:

Hebrews 6:6 [KJV]⁶If they shall fall away, to renew them again unto repentance; seeing they crucify to themselves the Son of God afresh, and put *him* to an open shame.

<u>What does this mean?</u> <u>Can a person lose their salvation?</u>

➤———— <u>Scripture Reference: Hebrews 6:1-12</u> ————≺

Introduction: Repentance is something we do after we are saved or regenerated by God the Holy Ghost/Spirit.

We have to receive Lord Jesus Christ into our lives first, before we can repent of our wrongdoings against God.

Unbelievers in/of Lord Jesus Christ are unable to repent of sins committed against God. Unbelievers do not have a desire to repent or admit to sinning against God.

The sixth chapter of Hebrews is dealing with born again believers in Lord Jesus Christ, it's referring to saved individuals, and we know this because it is emphasizing the repentance of an individual or people.

Being saved does not remove our ability to sin or transgress against God. We have a choice <u>not</u> to sin against God, if we depend on Lord Jesus Christ instead of ourselves to prevent us from sinning.

There is a difference in committing a sin against God through carelessness or ignorance and committing a sin willfully and knowingly against God.

<u>The title of this message from God is,</u> *"Every believer should dedicate his or her life to Lord Jesus Christ."*

Every believer should do whatever it takes to mature spiritually and become the best servant and witness unto Lord Jesus Christ that we can possibly be.

<u>In the scripture text God uses the Hebrews epistle (</u>*letter***<u>) to teach us three important facts about a believer's service unto God.</u>**

The first important fact about a believer's service unto God that God uses the Hebrews epistle to teach us is that, *"Living a godly lifestyle in Lord Jesus Christ is essential for spiritual maturity"*. A believer who willfully and knowingly sin against God will lose their testimony/witness.

Looking at Hebrews chapter 6, verses **1** thru **6**, we see that the scripture text says, "**Hebrews 6:1 - 6 [KJV]** ¹Therefore leaving the principles of the doctrine of Christ, let us go on unto perfection; not laying again the foundation of repentance from dead works, and of

faith toward God, ²Of the doctrine of baptisms, and of laying on of hands, and of resurrection of the dead, and of eternal judgment. ³And this will we do, if God permit. ⁴For *it is* impossible for those who were once enlightened, and have tasted of the heavenly gift, and were made partakers of the Holy Ghost, ⁵And have tasted the good word of God, and the powers of the world to come, ⁶If they shall fall away, to renew them again unto repentance; seeing they crucify to themselves the Son of God afresh, and put *him* to an open shame." The writer of the letter titled Hebrews wanted to move on to spiritual maturity for the readers, and not dwell on the things that even a new believer should already know. The scripture text lets us know that whenever a person who has been saved or regenerated by God the Holy Ghost, and also received sound doctrine or teaching about God and the things of God, but decides to continue to live the life of a sinner instead of a godly lifestyle in Lord Jesus Christ, then he or she will lose their testimony as a witness unto Lord Jesus Christ. A person who loses his or her testimony as a witness unto Lord Jesus Christ is worthless as a servant unto God, even if that person sincerely repents after willfully and knowingly sinning against God, they have made themselves useless unto God, because they purposely profaned the gospel of Lord Jesus Christ instead of obediently proclaiming the gospel of Lord Jesus Christ. Saved people who knowingly and willfully profane the name and gospel of Lord Jesus Christ will not lose their salvation, but they will preclude any chances of receiving a reward that will be given to the believers who are faithfully proclaiming the name and gospel of Lord Jesus Christ. The Hebrews epistle is written mainly to Jewish believers who struggle with the false doctrine or teaching that says a person has to also keep the Mosaic Law along with their belief/faith in Lord Jesus Christ.

Illustration: Back in the 1960s and/or 70s, there used to be a lot of television commercials claiming that margarine is better than butter. There were many people who believed the commercials and started using margarine instead of butter.

The Hebrews epistle is claiming that the Gospel of Lord Jesus Christ is superior and eliminates the Mosaic Law. The keeping of the Law for salvation after the resurrection and ascension of Lord Jesus Christ is a sin! The Gospel of Lord Jesus Christ is the new agreement or new covenant between God and mankind, which makes the old covenant obsolete. The Bible says, "**2 Corinthians 5:10 [KJV]** ¹⁰For we must all appear before the judgment seat of Christ; that every one may receive the things *done* in *his* body, according to that he hath done, whether *it be* good or bad." What this means for us is that there is still a judgment for believers, for obedience, not salvation. An unrepentant believer who willfully and knowingly continues to live their life as a sinner will cause God to eventually terminate his or her time on the earth. Physical death is a very good deterrent against a person who willfully and knowingly sin against God.

The next important fact about a believer's service unto God that God uses the Hebrews epistle to teach us is that, *"Lord Jesus Christ will judge every believer's faithfulness to do God's Will"*. Every believer who does God's Will on earth, will be rewarded in Heaven.

Looking again at the scripture text, verses **7** and **8** of the 6th chapter of Hebrews say, "**Hebrews 6:7 - 8 [KJV]** ⁷For the earth which drinketh in the rain that cometh oft upon it, and bringeth forth herbs meet for them by whom it is dressed, receiveth blessing from God: ⁸But that which beareth thorns and briers *is* rejected, and *is* nigh unto cursing; whose end *is* to be burned." The main or primary reason for Lord Jesus Christ leaving believers on the earth after being saved is to be used by Lord Jesus Christ to carry on the ministry that He started when He was on the earth. Every believer that allows Lord Jesus Christ to use him or her for ministry unto mankind is similar to the earth after receiving rain it produces plenty of herbs, fruits, and other vegetation that is useful to mankind. Lord Jesus Christ desire is to get plenty of use out of every one of us who is willing to be used as His servants.

Illustration: A young man decided one year to cut off all the dead looking limbs off of a grapefruit tree in his backyard. After he finished, the young man stood back from the tree to see how it looked. He had cut so much off of the tree that he thought the tree would die, but to his amazement the next time the tree bared fruit, it produced more grapefruits than it had ever produced before.

Lord Jesus Christ says, "**John 15:5 - 6 [KJV]** ⁵I am the vine, ye *are* the branches: He that abideth in me, and I in him, the same bringeth forth much fruit: for without me ye can do nothing. ⁶If a man abide not in me, he is cast forth as a branch, and is withered; and men gather them, and cast *them* into the fire, and they are burned." Every believer who refuses to mature spiritually and continue in a sinful lifestyle is similar to the earth producing thorns and briers after receiving rain. The Bible says, "**1 Corinthians 3:11 - 15 [KJV]** ¹¹For other foundation can no man lay than that is laid, which is Jesus Christ. ¹²Now if any man build upon this foundation gold, silver, precious stones, wood, hay, stubble; ¹³Every man's work shall be made manifest: for the day shall declare it, because it shall be revealed by fire; and the fire shall try every man's work of what sort it is. ¹⁴If any man's work abide which he hath built thereupon, he shall receive a reward. ¹⁵If any man's work shall be burned, he shall suffer loss: but he himself shall be saved; yet so as by fire." What this means for us is that salvation is not gotten by good works; otherwise a person could lose their salvation. Unfortunately there are people who will not serve Lord Jesus Christ after being saved; otherwise the Bible would not have mentioned this warning to us. The believers who refuse to serve Lord Jesus Christ will suffer loss for eternity, while those of us who choose to serve Lord Jesus Christ will be rewarded for eternity.

Not only does the Hebrews epistle make known to us that, *"Living a godly lifestyle in Lord Jesus Christ is essential for spiritual maturity"*, and that, *"Lord Jesus Christ will judge every believer's faithfulness to do God's Will"*. The Hebrews epistle also reveals to us that, *"Being a servant of Lord Jesus Christ is not a waste of time."* God has promised to reward all believers who are faithful servants.

Looking again for the last time at the scripture text, we see that verses **9** thru **12** of the 6th chapter of Hebrews says, "**Hebrews 6:9 - 12 [KJV]** ⁹But, beloved, we are persuaded better things of you, and things that accompany salvation, though we thus speak. ¹⁰For God *is* not unrighteous to forget your work and labour of love, which ye have showed toward his name, in that ye have ministered to the saints, and do minister. ¹¹And we desire that every one of you do show the same diligence to the full assurance of hope unto the end: ¹²That ye be not slothful, but followers of them who through faith and patience inherit the promises." We may not see any results from the things that God commission us to do, because what we do today or during our lifetime maybe for the benefit of someone who is born after we have experienced physical death or the Rapture. The scripture text is encouraging every believer to be the best servants unto Lord Jesus Christ that we possibly can, because God has promised to reward everyone who do so.

Illustration: At a high school graduation June the 2nd A.D. 2012 one of the speakers read off a list of careers and occupations as well as educational pursues that the graduating students were intending to do.

When it comes to being a servant unto Lord Jesus Christ we should learn as much as we possibly can about God, we should work as hard as Lord Jesus Christ desire us to work as His servants. Every believer should be more zealous about spiritual maturity and spiritual service than we are about secular education and secular jobs. What this means for us is that Almighty Holy God has made it perfectly clear that if we choose to be servants of Lord Jesus Christ, we will be rewarded for our efforts. If we have enough faith in Lord Jesus Christ for our salvation (*eternal life*), then we should have enough faith in Lord Jesus Christ to take advantage of the incentives that God is providing for every believer to be diligent and obedient servants of Lord Jesus Christ.

Conclusion: Now that we fully understand that, *"Every believer should dedicate his or her life to Lord Jesus Christ,"* and that every believer should do whatever it takes to mature spiritually and become the best servant and witness unto Lord Jesus Christ that we can possibly be.

What will we do in order for this to happen and continue to happen in our life on a continuous basis?

Will we finally give up our independent selfish desires and become selfless through our dependence on Lord Jesus Christ?

Will we take God at His word and earn as many of those rewards in Heaven/eternity that we can?

Will we make up our minds to be obedient unto God and do whatever He has told us to do?

2 Timothy 2:15 [KJV] ¹⁵Study to show thyself approved unto God, a workman that needeth not to be ashamed, rightly dividing the word of truth.

Notes and Reflection:

1 Peter 3:19 [KJV] ¹⁹By which also he went and preached unto the spirits in prison;

<u>What does this mean?</u> <u>Did Lord Jesus Christ go to Hell to preach to unbelievers in Hell</u>?

⟩—— <u>Scripture Reference: 1 Peter 3:13-22</u> ——⟨

Introduction: The Bible clearly teaches us that the evil world system that we live in will get worse instead of better. There will be deceptions and lies to make people believe and be deceived into thinking things are getting better, but this is only a cover up of the real evil that's being master minded against mankind by Satan the devil.

Not until Lord Jesus Christ returns to earth and set up His Millennium Kingdom will the World we live in take a turn for the better.

The title of this message from God is, *"Unjust suffering is the evidence that Lord Jesus Christ is living the Christian life through us."*

Unjust suffering is something that Lord Jesus Christ is very familiar with and will guide us through it.

In the scripture text God uses the Apostle Peter to teach us three important facts about Christian suffering.

The first important fact about Christian suffering that God uses the Apostle Peter to teach us is that, *"Every believer in Lord Jesus Christ should expect evil attacks for well-doing".* Everybody is suffering in this evil world system that we live in.

Looking at 1ˢᵗ Peter chapter 3, verses **13** thru **17**, we see that the scripture text says, "**1 Peter 3:13 - 17 [KJV]** ¹³And who *is* he that will harm you, if ye be followers of that which is good? ¹⁴But and if ye suffer for righteousness' sake, happy *are ye*: and be not afraid of their terror, neither be troubled; ¹⁵But sanctify the Lord God in your hearts: and *be* ready always to *give* an answer to every man that asketh you a reason of the hope that is in you with meekness and fear: ¹⁶Having a good conscience; that, whereas they speak evil of you, as of evildoers, they may be ashamed that falsely accuse your good conversation in Christ. ¹⁷For *it is* better, if the will of God be so, that ye suffer for well doing, than for evil doing." The scripture text is clearly saying that Christians should be peace makers instead of law breakers. Nowhere in the Bible does it teaches that once we become Christians; followers of Lord Jesus Christ, we will live happily ever after on the earth. The happily ever after comes after we go to Heaven. As believers in Lord Jesus Christ we have a choice that unbelievers do not have, we can choose to suffer for well doing or evil doing. The only choice the unbeliever has is to suffer for wrongdoing. Unbelievers automatically rebel against God and God's righteous standard of living; therefore from God's viewpoint they are evildoers doing wrong continuously. Before Almighty Holy God

intervened into our lives and revealed the truth to us about Lord Jesus Christ, and gave us the faith to believe in the saving grace of God, which is the sacrifice of Lord Jesus Christ for our salvation, we were on a path of self-destruction just like everybody else. Anytime a person refuses to follow Lord Jesus Christ and His teachings that are found in the Bible, then he or she is on a path of self-destruction.

<u>Illustration:</u> A man preparing for early retirement from the work force purchased a new air condition and heating unit to replace the ten years old less efficient unit, was deceived by the seller who installed the new unit. In an attempt to force a maintenance agreement from the buyer, the seller had to be called every summer to make the unit blow cold air instead of cool air. After the fourth year of this routine, the buyer called a Christian air condition maintenance company to look at the unit and the technician made the unit run the way it is supposed to run.

Satan the devil is using unsaved mankind and all the resources of the evil world system that we live in to keep unsaved mankind from the truth about Lord Jesus Christ and also to try and keep believers in Lord Jesus Christ from sharing the truth about Lord Jesus Christ to the unsaved/unbelievers. The devil has created many false religions and cults for unsaved mankind to participate in, as well as the theory of evolution to keep the unsaved from the truth about Lord Jesus Christ, and on the path of self-destruction with the different kinds of harmful drugs that are freely circulating in communities throughout the World. What this means for us is that Satan the devil is mobilizing unsaved mankind against believers in Lord Jesus Christ, by characterizing us as haters of humanity, so that no one will listen to the truth from us. Regardless of the suppression and oppression that the devil will use unsaved mankind to try to make our lives unbearable, and try to discredit what we say about Lord Jesus Christ, we have to be willing to suffer for praying out loud in the name of Jesus or fearlessly proclaiming the good news about Lord Jesus Christ. We need to let Lord Jesus Christ live through us by way of the Holy Ghost, so that our lives will bring glory unto God and live peaceable with other human beings.

The next important fact about Christian suffering that God uses the Apostle Peter to teach us is that, *"No human being has ever suffered more unjustly than Lord Jesus Christ"*. Lord Jesus Christ has suffered because of mankind even before His incarnation.

Looking again at the scripture text, verses **18** thru **20** of the 3rd chapter of 1st Peter say, "**1 Peter 3:18 - 20 [KJV]** ¹⁸**For Christ also hath once suffered for sins, the just for the unjust, that he might bring us to God, being put to death in the flesh, but quickened by the Spirit:** ¹⁹**By which also he went and preached unto the spirits in prison;** ²⁰**Which sometime were disobedient, when once the longsuffering of God waited in the days of Noah, while the ark was a preparing, wherein few, that is, eight souls were saved by water.**" Before Lord Jesus Christ died on the cross and was resurrected from the dead on the third day by the Holy Ghost/Spirit to pay the penalty for sin, the pre-incarnated Lord Jesus Christ was known as the **Word**, who was with God and is God, a member of the Triune Godhead.

<u>Illustration:</u> Past + Present + Future = time; The Father + The Son (*Lord Jesus Christ*) + The Holy Ghost/Spirit = The Triune Godhead.

The **Word** or pre-incarnated Lord Jesus Christ by way of the Holy Ghost/Spirit preached through Noah to the people for 120 years, all the while Noah was building the Ark. Unfortunately the wicked people of that day refused to believe the message God preached through Noah and they all died in the flood; their souls or spirits are in a holding place (*prison*) for evildoers waiting for the Great White Throne Judgment that will occur after the Millennium Kingdom. Only Noah, his wife, his three sons, and the wife of each of Noah's sons; a total of eight persons, lived through the flood. What this means for us is that Lord Jesus Christ has never went to Hades or the holding place for evil souls to preach to them, because if a person does not believe in God (*obey and worship*) during the Old Testament days or Lord Jesus Christ during the New Testament days before they experience physical death, then their eternal destination is permanently settled at that time. Believers will end up in Heaven for eternity and unbelievers will end up in the Lake of Fire for eternity.

Not only does the Apostle Peter make known to us that, *"Every believer in Lord Jesus Christ should expect evil attacks for well-doing"*, and that, *"No human being has ever suffered more unjustly than Lord Jesus Christ"*. The Apostle Peter also reveals to us that, *"Every believer has a new identity in Lord Jesus Christ."* The regeneration of the Holy Ghost/Spirit places every believer in the spiritual body of Lord Jesus Christ and under His authority.

Looking again for the last time at the scripture text, we see that verses **21** and **22** of the 3rd chapter of 1st Peter says, "**1 Peter 3:21 - 22 [KJV]** ^{21}The like figure whereunto *even* baptism doth also now save us (not the putting away of the filth of the flesh, but the answer of a good conscience toward God,) by the resurrection of Jesus Christ: ^{22}Who is gone into heaven, and is on the right hand of God; angels and authorities and powers being made subject unto him." The finished work of Lord Jesus Christ on the cross has provided many benefits for mankind. The baptism of the Holy Ghost/Spirit is probably the most important of the benefits for mankind, as a result of the finished work of Lord Jesus Christ on the cross. The baptism of the Holy Ghost is different from the baptism with water. The baptism with water is an outward expression of what has taken place in the inner person by the baptism of the Holy Ghost/Spirit. The baptism of the Holy Ghost is the process of regeneration that God the Holy Ghost causes to happen to a person, which changes a person's character towards God. The regeneration of God the Holy Ghost/Spirit causes a person's attitude towards God to change from a rebellious enemy to a cooperate friend that's willing to be an obedient servant unto God. The baptism of the Holy Ghost or regeneration of God the Holy Ghost, gives us the ability or power through Lord Jesus Christ to say no to our inherited sin nature that is hostile towards God and yes to God as an adopted child of God.

<u>Illustration:</u> A 15th century Bible translator was given the option of retracting what he wrote about salvation coming through faith instead of works, or suffer the consequence of being burned to death, the believer chose to be burned to death.

The Bible says, "**Acts 5:40-42 [KJV]** **⁴⁰And to him they agreed: and when they had called the apostles, and beaten *them*, they commanded that they should not speak in the name of Jesus, and let them go. ⁴¹ And they departed from the presence of the council, rejoicing that they were counted worthy to suffer shame for his name. ⁴² And daily in the temple, and in every house, they ceased not to teach and preach Jesus Christ.**" God protected Noah and his family from the destruction of mankind before the flood by putting them in the Ark, a very large boat; and today God is protecting believers from the destruction of evildoers and the evil world system that we live in by the baptism of the Holy Ghost that places us in the spiritual body of Lord Jesus Christ, called the Church. **What this means for us is that the baptism of the Holy Ghost saves us from condemnation and spending eternity in the Lake of Fire, and most of all, it changes our attitude and the way we think and feel about God.**

Conclusion: Now that we fully understand that, *"Unjust suffering is the evidence that Lord Jesus Christ is living the Christian life through us,"* and that unjust suffering is something that Lord Jesus Christ is very familiar with and will guide us through it.

What does the knowledge of expected unjust suffering means to us?

Can we finally see that unjust suffering or suffering for well-doing is an occasion for rejoicing not mourning and/or complaining?

Do we appreciate the long-suffering of God in the person of Lord Jesus Christ; even as the **Word** He suffered through the evil, non-repenting hearts/minds of mankind during the days of Noah?

Do we understand that salvation through Lord Jesus Christ is both a spiritual and physical rescue of believing mankind?

Notes and Reflection:

1 John 5:8 [KJV] ⁸And there are three that bear witness in earth, the Spirit, and the water, and the blood: and these three agree in one.

➤—— Scripture Reference: 1John 5:1-13 ——◄

Introduction: Secular history will admit that Lord Jesus Christ is a human being that lived and died on a cross by crucifixion, but we have to go to the biblical history of Lord Jesus Christ to know why He lived and was crucified on the cross.

We have to go to the biblical history of Lord Jesus Christ to find out that He also was resurrected from the dead/grave and that He lives forever as our everlasting High Priest, KING of Kings, LORD of Lords, and the master of our service.

The question before us is, *"Do we believe what the Bible says about Lord Jesus Christ?"* Do we believe that Lord Jesus Christ is the Messiah; the Savior of mankind, or just a good person who made wonderful speeches?

The title of this message from God is, *"Lord Jesus Christ died on the cross for the sins of mankind."*

Every person has to believe in the death, burial, and resurrection of Lord Jesus Christ in order to be saved.

In the scripture text God uses the Apostle John to teach us three important facts about salvation.

The first important fact about salvation that God uses the Apostle John to teach us is that, *"The evil world system that we live in is defeated by our belief in Lord Jesus Christ".* Faith in Lord Jesus Christ is the believer's ultimate weapon against evil and evildoers.

Looking at 1ˢᵗ John chapter 5, verses **1** thru **5**, we see that the scripture text says, **1 John 5:1 - 5 [KJV]** ¹Whosoever believeth that Jesus is the Christ is born of God: and every one that loveth him that begat loveth him also that is begotten of him. ²By this we know that we love the children of God, when we love God, and keep his commandments. ³For this is the love of God, that we keep his commandments: and his commandments are not grievous. ⁴For whatsoever is born of God overcometh the world: and this is the victory that overcometh the world, *even* our faith. ⁵Who is he that overcometh the world, but he that believeth that Jesus is the Son of God? The scripture text tells us that a born again believer is someone who believes that Lord Jesus Christ is the Anointed One or Messiah; the Savior of mankind sent by/ from God. Three things that the indwelling of God the Holy Ghost/Spirit does for us, is give us the ability to love God the Father; the ability to love God the Son who is our Lord and Savior Jesus Christ; and also the ability to love all the other believers who are spiritually connected to each other and Lord Jesus Christ by way of the Holy Ghost/Spirit.

Back in the late 1950s thru the early 1960s when the United States of America had great respect for God and the name of Lord Jesus Christ, as a child we used multipurpose oil on our bicycle chains when they got rusty and also to lubricate a plethora of other things. The name of the multipurpose oil was, "*3 in 1 oil*".

Almighty Holy God is Three in One. God is a Trinity; the Father, Son, and Holy Ghost. Every member of the Triune Godhead is instrumental for the salvation of mankind. God the Father is the One who calls unbelievers to Lord Jesus Christ. The Bible tells us what Lord Jesus Christ says, **"John 6:65 [KJV]** [65]And he said, Therefore said I unto you, that no man can come unto me, except it were given unto him of my Father." God the Father gives us the faith we need to trust and believe in Lord Jesus Christ. God the Holy Ghost changes our attitude/mind towards God. The Bible says, **"Titus 3:5 [KJV]** [5]Not by works of righteousness which we have done, but according to his mercy he saved us, by the washing of regeneration, and renewing of the Holy Ghost;" Lord Jesus Christ died a substitutionary death for mankind on the cross. **"John 14:6 [KJV]** [6]Jesus saith unto him, I am the way, the truth, and the life: no man cometh unto the Father, but by me." What this means for us is that the Triune Godhead or God, is responsible for our salvation. Each member of the Trinity is equally active in the redemption of mankind. Love for God and obedience unto God is something that only believers in Lord Jesus Christ can do.

The next important fact about salvation that God uses the Apostle John to teach us is that, *"God in the person of Lord Jesus Christ did exactly what He came into the World to do"*. The proof of Lord Jesus Christ's accomplishment or finished work on the cross is undeniable.

Looking again at the scripture text, verses **6** thru **10** of the 5th chapter of 1st John say, **1 John 5:6 - 10 [KJV]** [6]This is he that came by water and blood, *even* Jesus Christ; not by water only, but by water and blood. And it is the Spirit that beareth witness, because the Spirit is truth. [7]For there are three that bear record in heaven, the Father, the Word, and the Holy Ghost: and these three are one. [8]And there are three that bear witness in earth, the Spirit, and the water, and the blood: and these three agree in one. [9]If we receive the witness of men, the witness of God is greater: for this is the witness of God which he hath testified of his Son. [10]He that believeth on the Son of God hath the witness in himself: he that believeth not God hath made him a liar; because he believeth not the record that God gave of his Son. According to the Old Testament under the Mosaic Law, a person could be put to death with a minimum of two or three witnesses. One witness was not enough to cause a person to be put to death. The Bible says, **"Deuteronomy 17:6 [KJV]** [6]At the mouth of two witnesses, or three witnesses, shall he that is worthy of death be put to death; *but* at the mouth of one witness he shall not be put to death." Unfortunately in a fallen World full of lies and deceit, we need to have witnesses to determine who is really telling the truth.

In a children molestation trial of an assistance football coach of a well-known university in the United States of America, it took about 8 to 12 witnesses/victims to get a conviction.

Lord Jesus Christ says in the Bible, "**Matthew 18:16 [KJV]** ¹⁶But if he will not hear *thee,* *then* take with thee one or two more, that in the mouth of two or three witnesses every word may be established." The proof that Lord Jesus Christ died on the cross is important for His claims that He would rise from the dead/grave three days later. The Bible tells us what God says about blood, "**Leviticus 17:11 [KJV]** ¹¹For the life of the flesh *is* in the blood: and I have given it to you upon the altar to make an atonement for your souls: for it *is* the blood *that* maketh an atonement for the soul." The Apostle John saw or witnessed the blood and also the water that came out of Lord Jesus Christ when the Roman soldier thrust a spear in Lord Jesus Christ's side to prove that He was dead. Water also represents the written word of God that's found in the Bible; the whole Bible is a witness unto Lord Jesus Christ. **What this means for us is that the Apostle John and other people at the crucifixion of Lord Jesus Christ saw Lord Jesus Christ die on the cross, and the Apostle John tells us about the two main elements needed to sustain human life coming out of His body when the Roman soldier thrust a spear into the side of Lord Jesus Christ. And if that's not enough, we have the ultimate witness of the Triune Godhead. The Apostle John is also one of many who saw the resurrected Lord Jesus Christ. These are things we have to believe in order for us to be saved.**

Not only does the Apostle John make known to us that, *"The evil world system that we live in is defeated by our belief in Lord Jesus Christ"*, and that, *"God in the person of Lord Jesus Christ did exactly what He came into the World to do"*. The Apostle John also reveals to us that, *"Salvation is a relationship with Lord Jesus Christ."* A personal relationship with Lord Jesus Christ is the only way a person can be saved.

Looking again for the last time at the scripture text, we see that verses **11** thru **13** of the 5th chapter of 1st John say, **1 John 5:11 - 13 [KJV]** ¹¹And this is the record, that God hath given to us eternal life, and this life is in his Son. ¹²He that hath the Son hath life; *and* he that hath not the Son of God hath not life. ¹³These things have I written unto you that believe on the name of the Son of God; that ye may know that ye have eternal life, and that ye may believe on the name of the Son of God.

Illustration: An older man said to a younger man that he prefers to depend on a short pencil instead of a long memory.

The Apostle John says that he wrote this letter/epistle so that believers could know for certain that if they believe in or on the name of Lord Jesus Christ, they have eternal life, which means they have a place in Heaven with God forever. Believing in the name of Lord Jesus Christ is the same as believing in the person Himself. What this means for us is that if Lord Jesus Christ is not living the Christian life through us by way of the Holy Ghost, then there is a strong possibility that we are not saved yet. We have to decrease in order for Lord Jesus Christ to increase in our lives, and God the Holy Ghost gives us the ability to do that.

Conclusion: Now that we fully understand that, *"Lord Jesus Christ died on the cross for the sins of mankind,"* and that every person has to believe in the death, burial, and resurrection of Lord Jesus Christ in order to be saved.

What do we think about the truth God has revealed to us through the Apostle John about salvation?

Do we have abundant life through Lord Jesus Christ or do we allow the evil world system and evildoers take away our joy of life?

Do we believe that Lord Jesus Christ experienced physical death on the cross for our salvation and rose from the grave/dead for our justification?

Do we know for certain that we have Lord Jesus Christ in our life or is it still something that we are hoping for?

Notes and Reflection:

Chapter 4: Not in the Bible.

"Cleanliness is next to godliness"

This is not a scripture verse from the Bible. Because of a failure to read and study the whole Bible many professing Christians do not know that this is not a Bible verse; therefore many new believers hear older local church members use this phrase like scripture from the Bible and also start using it in the same manner.

The Golden Rule, *"Do unto others as you would have them to do unto you,"* is found in the Bible. **Matthew 7:12 [KJV]** [12] Therefore all things whatsoever ye would that men should do to you, do ye even so to them: for this is the law and the prophets.

In order for us to know what's in the Bible and what's not in the Bible, we need to read every word of the Bible, preferably in the order that it is written from the beginning to the end, to preclude a multitude of voids in a believer's learning.

Cleanliness is something that all believers should embrace, but it should never be viewed as a prerequisite for salvation or a duty to maintain salvation.

For example: The Bible says, "**Matthew 25:31-46 [KJV]** [31] When the Son of man shall come in his glory, and all the holy angels with him, then shall he sit upon the throne of his glory: [32] And before him shall be gathered all nations: and he shall separate them one from another, as a shepherd divideth *his* sheep from the goats: [33] And he shall set the sheep on his right hand, but the goats on the left. [34] Then shall the King say unto them on his right hand, Come, ye blessed of my Father, inherit the kingdom prepared for you from the foundation of the world: [35] For I was an hungred, and ye gave me meat: I was thirsty, and ye gave me drink: I was a stranger, and ye took me in: [36] Naked, and ye clothed me: I was sick, and ye visited me: I was in prison, and ye came unto me. [37] Then shall the righteous answer him, saying, Lord, when saw we thee an hungred, and fed *thee*? or thirsty, and gave *thee* drink? [38] When saw we thee a stranger, and took *thee* in? or naked, and clothed *thee*? [39] Or when saw we thee sick, or in prison, and came unto thee? [40] And the King shall answer and say unto them, Verily I say unto you, Inasmuch as ye have done *it* unto one of the least of these my brethren, ye have done *it* unto me. [41] Then shall he say also unto them on the left hand, Depart from me, ye cursed, into everlasting fire, prepared for the devil and his angels: [42] For I was an hungred, and ye gave me no meat: I was thirsty, and ye gave me no drink: [43] I was a stranger, and ye took me not in: naked, and ye clothed me not: sick, and in prison, and ye visited me not. [44] Then shall they also answer him, saying, Lord, when saw we thee an hungred, or athirst, or a stranger, or naked, or sick, or in prison, and did not minister unto thee? [45] Then shall he answer them, saying, Verily I say unto you, Inasmuch as ye did *it* not to one of the least of these, ye did *it* not to me. [46] And these shall go away into everlasting punishment: but the righteous into life eternal."

Many preachers and Bible teachers have falsely preached and taught that in order for a person to be saved and keep their salvation, they have to do what the above scripture says. These are things that Lord Jesus Christ will do through believers by way of the Holy Ghost because we are saved. God the Holy Ghost/Spirit indwells every believer. The indwelling of the Holy Ghost is our guarantee that we are saved, because His presence in us means that we have a relationship with Lord Jesus Christ.

Lord Jesus Christ said the above scripture during the Law Dispensation. Under the Law a person was either blessed or cursed depending on their obedience unto God. Those individuals who died under or during the Law Dispensation will be subject to this separation or judgment.

Everybody who is saved after the death, burial, and resurrection of Lord Jesus Christ is under the Dispensation of Grace.

Ephesians 3:2 [KJV] [2]If ye have heard of the dispensation of the grace of God which is given me to you-ward:

The letters of the Apostle Paul give us the details about the Church and the Grace Dispensation. If we obey God under or during the Grace Dispensation we will receive a reward(s) in Heaven. If we disobey God we will suffer loss in Heaven for eternity.

1 Corinthians 3:8-15 [KJV] [8] Now he that planteth and he that watereth are one: and every man shall receive his own reward according to his own labour. [9] For we are labourers together with God: ye are God's husbandry, *ye are* God's building. [10] According to the grace of God which is given unto me, as a wise masterbuilder, I have laid the foundation, and another buildeth thereon. But let every man take heed how he buildeth thereupon. [11] For other foundation can no man lay than that is laid, which is Jesus Christ. [12] Now if any man build upon this foundation gold, silver, precious stones, wood, hay, stubble; [13] Every man's work shall be made manifest: for the day shall declare it, because it shall be revealed by fire; and the fire shall try every man's work of what sort it is. [14] If any man's work abide which he hath built thereupon, he shall receive a <u>reward</u>. [15] If any man's work shall be burned, he shall <u>suffer loss</u>: but he himself shall be saved; yet so as by fire.

We cannot lose our salvation under Grace, because our salvation depends on what Lord Jesus Christ has done for us on the cross; for us it is unconditional. Lord Jesus Christ chose to save us, therefore we are saved by grace through faith in Him; never for what we do or do not do. Our obedience unto God affects eternal rewards in Heaven and blessings on Earth only.

The Law is conditional; dependent on/upon a person's obedience unto God. We are not under the Law!

We should never use the saying or phrase, *"Cleanliness is next to godliness"* as if it is Bible scripture or something we <u>must</u> do to be saved and also in order for us not to lose our salvation.

Notes and Reflection:

"God helps those who help themselves"

This is a saying or phrase that's not in the Bible. Unfortunately this saying has many negative usages in the local churches. It has been used in the local churches to solicit money from the congregation. In other words, if you give to God, then God will give to you. Accompanied by the phrases, *"You can't beat God giving"* and *"You can't beat God taking"*, many professing Christians because of a failure to read and study the whole Bible are forced/lead to believe that in order to receive blessings from God we must first give our money to the local church, and if we do not give to the local church, then God will take what we have and leave us broke or homeless.

Not only does this phrase or saying teach new believers the false doctrine of you must first give to God through the local church to receive from God, it also allows make-believers (*unbelievers pretending to be saved*) to keep their money all to themselves. If a poor homeless person in need of some sincere help ask for help from the local church, the make-believers will use this saying to justify not helping those in need.

The Bible clearly teaches that Lord Jesus Christ died on the cross and rose from the grave because totally corrupt mankind is unable to help ourselves! Spiritually mature believers understand the doctrine the Bible teaches on the total depravity of mankind before the intervention of Lord Jesus Christ into our lives. According to the Bible we are saved by God's grace or unearned kindness through the faith that God gives us to believe.

> **Ephesians 2:8-10 [KJV]** **8**For by grace are ye saved through faith; and that not of your-selves: *it is* the gift of God: **9** Not of works, lest any man should boast. **10** For we are his work-manship, created in Christ Jesus unto good works, which God hath before ordained that we should walk in them.

> **Romans 12:3 [KJV]** **3** For I say, through the grace given unto me, to every man that is among you, not to think *of himself* more highly than he ought to think; but to think sober-ly, according as God hath dealt to every man the measure of faith.

Our salvation is totally from God in the person of Lord Jesus Christ, all we do is accept the salvation of God's irresistible grace with the measure of faith that God has given us. We did absolutely nothing to be saved, except believe.

> **John 6:47 [KJV]** **47** Verily, verily, I say unto you, He that believeth on me hath everlasting life.

The phrase, *"God helps those who help themselves"* is unbiblical as a Bible concept and it's not found in the Bible. We need to discourage the use of phrases or sayings like this by professing Christians.

Notes and Reflection:

Chapter 5: Synchronizing the four accounts of the Gospel.

This is an attempt to use all four accounts of the gospel to get a more complete detail account about the trial, crucifixion, and resurrection of Lord Jesus Christ.

Luke 22:7 - 13 [KJV] ⁷Then came the day of unleavened bread, when the passover must be killed. ⁸And he sent Peter and John, saying, Go and prepare us the passover, that we may eat. ⁹And they said unto him, Where wilt thou that we prepare? ¹⁰And he said unto them, Behold, when ye are entered into the city, there shall a man meet you, bearing a pitcher of water; follow him into the house where he entereth in. ¹¹And ye shall say unto the goodman of the house, The Master saith unto thee, Where is the guestchamber, where I shall eat the passover with my disciples? ¹²And he shall show you a large upper room furnished: there make ready. ¹³And they went, and found as he had said unto them: and they made ready the passover.

Lord Jesus Christ had attended other Passovers, but this one would be different from the others, because it would be the last Passover that would be acceptable unto God. During this last acceptable Passover Lord Jesus Christ started the observance of the Communion in place of the Passover.

John 13:21 - 30 [KJV] ²¹When Jesus had thus said, he was troubled in spirit, and testified, and said, Verily, verily, I say unto you, that one of you shall betray me. ²²Then the disciples looked one on another, doubting of whom he spake. ²³Now there was leaning on Jesus' bosom one of his disciples, whom Jesus loved. ²⁴Simon Peter therefore beckoned to him, that he should ask who it should be of whom he spake. ²⁵He then lying on Jesus' breast saith unto him, Lord, who is it? ²⁶Jesus answered, He it is, to whom I shall give a sop, when I have dipped *it*. And when he had dipped the sop, he gave *it* to Judas Iscariot, *the son* of Simon. ²⁷And after the sop Satan entered into him. Then said Jesus unto him, That thou doest, do quickly. ²⁸Now no man at the table knew for what intent he spake this unto him. ²⁹For some *of them* thought, because Judas had the bag, that Jesus had said unto him, Buy *those things* that we have need of against the feast; or, that he should give something to the poor. ³⁰He then having received the sop went immediately out: and it was night.

Lord Jesus Christ predicts the betrayal of one of His chosen disciples, and He tells John exactly who it is. It appears that Judas Iscariot left with Lord Jesus Christ's permission during the Passover meal.

Matthew 26:26 - 56 [KJV] ²⁶And as they were eating, Jesus took bread, and blessed *it*, and brake *it*, and gave *it* to the disciples, and said, Take, eat; this is my body. ²⁷And he took the cup, and gave thanks, and gave *it* to them, saying, Drink ye all of it; ²⁸For this is my blood of the new testament, which is shed for many for the remission of sins. ²⁹But I say unto you, I will not drink henceforth of this fruit of the vine, until that day when I drink it new with you in my Father's kingdom. ³⁰And when they had sung an hymn, they went out into the mount of Olives. ³¹Then saith Jesus unto them, All ye shall be offended because of me this night: for it is written, I will smite the shepherd, and the sheep of the flock shall be scattered abroad. [32]But after I am risen again, I will go before you into Galilee. [33]Peter answered and said unto him, Though all *men* shall be offended because of thee, *yet* will I never be offended. [34]Jesus said unto him, Verily I say unto thee, That this night, before the cock crow, thou shalt deny me thrice. [35]Peter said unto him, Though I should die with thee, yet will I not deny thee. Likewise also said all the disciples. [36]Then cometh Jesus with them unto a place called Gethsemane, and saith unto the disciples, Sit ye here, while I go and pray yonder. [37]And he took with him Peter and the two sons of Zebedee, and began to be sorrowful and very heavy. [38]Then saith he unto them, My soul is exceeding sorrowful, even unto death: tarry ye here, and watch with me. [39]And he went a little further, and fell on his face, and prayed, saying, O my Father, if it be possible, let this cup pass from me: nevertheless not as I will, but as thou *wilt*. [40]And he cometh unto the disciples, and findeth them asleep, and saith unto Peter, What, could ye not watch with me one hour? [41]Watch and pray, that ye enter not into temptation: the spirit indeed *is* willing, but the flesh *is* weak. [42]He went away again the second time, and prayed, saying, O my Father, if this cup may not pass away from me, except I drink it, thy will be done. [43]And he came and found them asleep again: for their eyes were heavy. [44]And he left them, and went away again, and prayed the third time, saying the same words. [45]Then cometh he to his disciples, and saith unto them, Sleep on now, and take *your* rest: behold, the hour is at hand, and the Son of man is betrayed into the hands of sinners. [46]Rise, let us be going: behold, he is at hand that doth betray me. [47]And while he yet spake, lo, Judas, one of the twelve, came, and with him a great multitude with swords and staves, from the chief priests and elders of the people. [48]Now he that betrayed him gave them a sign, saying, Whomsoever I shall kiss, that same is he: hold him fast. [49]And forthwith he came to Jesus, and said, Hail, master; and kissed him. [50]And Jesus said unto him, Friend, wherefore art thou come? Then came they, and laid hands on Jesus, and took him. [51]And, behold, one of them which were with Jesus stretched out *his* hand, and drew his sword, and struck a servant of the high priest's, and smote off his ear. [52]Then said Jesus unto him, Put up again thy sword into his place: for all they that take the sword shall perish with the sword. [53]Thinkest thou that I cannot now pray to my Father, and he shall presently give me more than twelve legions of angels? [54]But how then shall the scriptures be fulfilled, that thus it must be? [55]In that same hour said Jesus to the multitudes, Are ye come out as against a thief with swords and staves for to take me? I sat daily with you teaching in the temple, and ye laid no hold on me. [56]But all this was done, that the scriptures of the prophets might be fulfilled. Then all the disciples forsook him, and fled.

Lord Jesus Christ prays three times to God the Father concerning the physical sacrifice of His body that He was about to make for the salvation of believing mankind. He also predicted that Peter would deny Him three times before the night was over. Judas Iscariot betrayed Lord Jesus Christ with a kiss. One of the other gospel accounts let us know that it was Peter who cut off the right ear of Malcus and that Lord Jesus Christ touched Malcus and healed his ear right then and there.

John 18:12 - 23 [KJV] [12]Then the band and the captain and officers of the Jews took Jesus, and bound him, [13]And led him away to Annas first; for he was father in law to Caiaphas, which was the high priest that same year. [14]Now Caiaphas was he, which gave counsel to the Jews, that it was expedient that one man should die for the people. [15]And Simon Peter followed Jesus, and *so did* another disciple: that disciple was known unto the high priest, and went in with Jesus into the palace of the high priest. ¹⁶But Peter stood at the door without. Then went out that other disciple, which was known unto the high priest, and spake unto her that kept the door, and brought in Peter. ¹⁷Then saith the damsel that kept the door unto Peter, Art not thou also *one* of this man's disciples? He saith, I am not. ¹⁸And the servants and officers stood there, who had made a fire of coals; for it was cold: and they warmed themselves: and Peter stood with them, and warmed himself. ¹⁹The high priest then asked Jesus of his disciples, and of his doctrine. ²⁰Jesus answered him, I spake openly to the world; I ever taught in the synagogue, and in the temple, whither the Jews always resort; and in secret have I said nothing. ²¹Why askest thou me? ask them which heard me, what I have said unto them: behold, they know what I said. ²²And when he had thus spoken, one of the officers which stood by struck Jesus with the palm of his hand, saying, Answerest thou the high priest so? ²³Jesus answered him, If I have spoken evil, bear witness of the evil: but if well, why smitest thou me?

Peter and John followed as they took Lord Jesus Christ to face the religious rulers. John knew the High Priest and was able the get Peter inside the palace of the high priest. It was inside the palace of the high priest that Peter denied Lord Jesus Christ three times as predicted by Lord Jesus Christ. One of the officers slapped Lord Jesus Christ because he didn't like the way Lord Jesus Christ was speaking to the high priest.

Matthew 26:57 - 68 [KJV] ⁵⁷And they that had laid hold on Jesus led *him* away to Caiaphas the high priest, where the scribes and the elders were assembled. ⁵⁸But Peter followed him afar off unto the high priest's palace, and went in, and sat with the servants, to see the end. ⁵⁹Now the chief priests, and elders, and all the council, sought false witness against Jesus, to put him to death; ⁶⁰But found none: yea, though many false witnesses came, *yet* found they none. At the last came two false witnesses, ⁶¹And said, This *fellow* said, I am able to destroy the temple of God, and to build it in three days. ⁶²And the high priest arose, and said unto him, Answerest thou nothing? what *is it which* these witness against thee? ⁶³But Jesus held his peace. And the high priest answered and said unto him, I adjure thee by the living God, that thou tell us whether thou be the Christ, the Son of God. ⁶⁴Jesus saith unto him, Thou hast said: nevertheless I say unto you, Hereafter shall ye see the Son of man sitting on the right hand of power, and coming in the clouds of heaven. ⁶⁵Then the high priest rent his clothes, saying, He hath spoken blasphemy; what further need have we of witnesses? behold, now ye have heard his blasphemy. ⁶⁶What think ye? They answered and said, He is guilty of death. ⁶⁷Then did they spit in his face, and buffeted him; and others smote *him* with the palms of their hands, ⁶⁸Saying, Prophesy unto us, thou Christ, Who is he that smote thee?

This is repetitious of John 18:12-23, but it has more information of what happened. Lord Jesus Christ knew exactly what they were planning to do, so He refused to defend Himself so that it would be known that nobody could accuse Him of any wrongdoings. Even those who tried to lie on Him could not make a lie stick to Lord Jesus Christ. Lord Jesus Christ confesses that He is the Son of God and they said that He had spoken blasphemy which is punishable by death. Then they started beating on Him.

John 18:28 - 38 [KJV] ²⁸Then led they Jesus from Caiaphas unto the hall of judgment: and it was early; and they themselves went not into the judgment hall, lest they should be defiled; but that they might eat the passover. ²⁹Pilate then went out unto them, and said, What accusation bring ye against this man? ³⁰They answered and said unto him, If he were not a malefactor, we would not have delivered him up unto thee. ³¹Then said Pilate unto them, Take ye him, and judge him according to your law. The Jews therefore said unto him, It is not lawful for us to put any man to death: ³²That the saying of Jesus might be fulfilled, which he spake, signifying what death he should die. ³³Then Pilate entered into the judgment hall again, and called Jesus, and said unto him, Art thou the King of the Jews? ³⁴Jesus answered him, Sayest thou this thing of thyself, or did others tell it thee of me? ³⁵Pilate answered, Am I a Jew? Thine own nation and the chief priests have delivered thee unto me: what hast thou done? ³⁶Jesus answered, My kingdom is not of this world: if my kingdom were of this world, then would my servants fight, that I should not be delivered to the Jews: but now is my kingdom not from hence. ³⁷Pilate therefore said unto him, Art thou a king then? Jesus answered, Thou sayest that I am a king. To this end was I born, and for this cause came I into the world, that I should bear witness unto the truth. Every one that is of the truth heareth my voice. ³⁸Pilate saith unto him, What is truth? And when he had said this, he went out again unto the Jews, and saith unto them, I find in him no fault *at all*.

The Gospel account according to John is written in chronological order, which causes us to wonder how it is that Lord Jesus Christ and His disciples had the Passover meal in chapter 13, but the religious leaders and the rest of the Jews that followed the corrupt religious leaders had not had it yet. We know beyond the shadow of a doubt that Lord Jesus Christ and His disciples kept the Passover at the proper time. According to the book of Genesis, God created a day to start at evening, and then there is daylight and evening again which is the beginning of the next day. **Leviticus 23:5 [KJV]** ⁵In the fourteenth *day* of the first month at even is the LORD'S passover. *Lord Jesus Christ and His disciple kept the Passover according to God's definition of a day. The religious rulers and the Jews that followed them were keeping the Passover according to the Romans definition of day, from 12 midnight to 12 midnight which caused them to keep the Passover a day later than they should. Therefore Lord Jesus Christ the Lamb of God, died (experienced physical death) on the true Passover day!*

Luke 23:6 - 12 [KJV] ⁶When Pilate heard of Galilee, he asked whether the man were a Galilaean. ⁷And as soon as he knew that he belonged unto Herod's jurisdiction, he sent him to Herod, who himself also was at Jerusalem at that time. ⁸And when Herod saw Jesus, he was exceeding glad: for he was desirous to see him of a long *season*, because he had heard many things of him; and he hoped to have seen some miracle done by him. ⁹Then he questioned with him in many words; but he answered him nothing. ¹⁰And the chief priests and scribes stood and vehemently accused him. ¹¹And Herod with his men of war set him at nought, and mocked *him*, and arrayed him in a gorgeous robe, and sent him again to Pilate. ¹²And the same day Pilate and Herod were made friends together: for before they were at enmity between themselves.

An old saying, "The enemy of my enemy is my friend". Two corrupted individuals became friends because neither one of them had any reverence for Lord Jesus Christ.

Mark 15:6 - 32 [KJV] [6]Now at *that* feast he released unto them one prisoner, whomsoever they desired. [7]And there was *one* named Barabbas, *which lay* bound with them that had made insurrection with him, who had committed murder in the insurrection. [8]And the multitude crying aloud began to desire *him to do* as he had ever done unto them. [9]But Pilate answered them, saying, Will ye that I release unto you the King of the Jews? [10]For he knew that the chief priests had delivered him for envy. [11]But the chief priests moved the people, that he should rather release Barabbas unto them. [12]And Pilate answered and said again unto them, What will ye then that I shall do *unto him* whom ye call the King of the Jews? [13]And they cried out again, Crucify him. [14]Then Pilate said unto them, Why, what evil hath he done? And they cried out the more exceedingly, Crucify him. [15]And *so* Pilate, willing to content the people, released Barabbas unto them, and delivered Jesus, when he had scourged *him*, to be crucified. [16]And the soldiers led him away into the hall, called Praetorium; and they call together the whole band. [17]And they clothed him with purple, and platted a crown of thorns, and put it about his *head*, [18]And began to salute him, Hail, King of the Jews! [19]And they smote him on the head with a reed, and did spit upon him, and bowing *their* knees worshipped him. [20]And when they had mocked him, they took off the purple from him, and put his own clothes on him, and led him out to crucify him. [21]And they compel one Simon a Cyrenian, who passed by, coming out of the country, the father of Alexander and Rufus, to bear his cross. [22]And they bring him unto the place Golgotha, which is, being interpreted, The place of a skull. [23]And they gave him to drink wine mingled with myrrh: but he received *it* not. [24]And when they had crucified him, they parted his garments, casting lots upon them, what every man should take. [25]And it was the third hour, and they crucified him. [26]And the superscription of his accusation was written over, THE KING OF THE JEWS. [27]And with him they crucify two thieves; the one on his right hand, and the other on his left. [28]And the scripture was fulfilled, which saith, And he was numbered with the transgressors. [29]And they that passed by railed on him, wagging their heads, and saying, Ah, thou that destroyest the temple, and buildest *it* in three days, [30]Save thyself, and come down from the cross. [31]Likewise also the chief priests mocking said among themselves with the scribes, He saved others; himself he cannot save. [32]Let Christ the King of Israel descend now from the cross, that we may see and believe. And they that were crucified with him reviled him.

Lord Jesus Christ an innocent man being chosen to die instead of Barabbas the guilty man is symbolic of Lord Jesus Christ dying to free believing mankind from the sin debt that we owe to Almighty Holy God. Once again we get a glimpse of how much God loves mankind by the amount of physical abuse and verbal humiliation that Lord Jesus Christ endured on our behalf, being God He could have made His tormentors suffer, but He will do that at a later date to those who refuse to believe in Him.

Luke 23:39- 45 [KJV] ³⁹And one of the malefactors which were hanged railed on him, saying, If thou be Christ, save thyself and us. ⁴⁰But the other answering rebuked him, saying, Dost not thou fear God, seeing thou art in the same condemnation? ⁴¹And we indeed justly; for we receive the due reward of our deeds: but this man hath done nothing amiss. ⁴²And he said unto Jesus, Lord, remember me when thou comest into thy kingdom. ⁴³And Jesus said unto him, Verily I say unto thee, To day shalt thou be with me in paradise. ⁴⁴And it was about the sixth hour, and there was a darkness over all the earth until the ninth hour. ⁴⁵And the sun was darkened, and the veil of the temple was rent in the midst.

Now we can clearly see that salvation is not earned or deserved, by the fact that Lord Jesus Christ gave salvation to a man who simply believed that Lord Jesus Christ is whom He claimed to be. The man believed in Lord Jesus Christ by putting his faith and trust in Lord Jesus Christ for a better life after experiencing physical death. This man had no opportunity to do any good deeds or somehow get right with God before accepting the free gift of eternal life that is available only through Lord Jesus Christ.

John 19:28 - 41 [KJV] ²⁸After this, Jesus knowing that all things were now accomplished, that the scripture might be fulfilled, saith, I thirst. ²⁹Now there was set a vessel full of vinegar: and they filled a sponge with vinegar, and put *it* upon hyssop, and put *it* to his mouth. ³⁰When Jesus therefore had received the vinegar, he said, It is finished: and he bowed his head, and gave up the ghost. ³¹The Jews therefore, because it was the preparation, that the bodies should not remain upon the cross on the sabbath day, (for that sabbath day was an high day,) besought Pilate that their legs might be broken, and *that* they might be taken away. ³²Then came the soldiers, and brake the legs of the first, and of the other which was crucified with him. ³³But when they came to Jesus, and saw that he was dead already, they brake not his legs: ³⁴But one of the soldiers with a spear pierced his side, and forthwith came there out blood and water. ³⁵And he that saw *it* bare record, and his record is true: and he knoweth that he saith true, that ye might believe. ³⁶For these things were done, that the scripture should be fulfilled, A bone of him shall not be broken. ³⁷And again another scripture saith, They shall look on him whom they pierced. ³⁸And after this Joseph of Arimathaea, being a disciple of Jesus, but secretly for fear of the Jews, besought Pilate that he might take away the body of Jesus: and Pilate gave *him* leave. He came therefore, and took the body of Jesus. ³⁹And there came also Nicodemus, which at the first came to Jesus by night, and brought a mixture of myrrh and aloes, about an hundred pound *weight*. ⁴⁰Then took they the body of Jesus, and wound it in linen clothes with the spices, as the manner of the Jews is to bury. ⁴¹Now in the place where he was crucified there was a garden; and in the garden a new sepulchre, wherein was never man yet laid.

God in the person of Lord Jesus Christ came into this World that He created to provide salvation for believing mankind so that we won't be casted into the Lake of Fire with Satan the devil and the other fallen angels. God also proves to us that the Bible is true by the constant fulfilments of the things that were prophesized a long time ago.

Matthew 27:60 - 66 [KJV] [60]And laid it in his own new tomb, which he had hewn out in the rock: and he rolled a great stone to the door of the sepulchre, and departed. [61]And there was Mary Magdalene, and the other Mary, sitting over against the sepulchre. [62]Now the next day, that followed the day of the preparation, the chief priests and Pharisees came together unto Pilate, [63]Saying, Sir, we remember that that deceiver said, while he was yet alive, After three days I will rise again. [64]Command therefore that the sepulchre be made sure until the third day, lest his disciples come by night, and steal him away, and say unto the people, He is risen from the dead: so the last error shall be worse than the first. [65]Pilate said unto them, Ye have a watch: go your way, make *it* as sure as ye can. [66]So they went, and made the sepulchre sure, sealing the stone, and setting a watch.

Now we see that the wicked religious leaders understood some of the things Lord Jesus Christ was preaching and teaching but they refused to believe that He was telling the truth. A liar will assume that other people are liars also. By having the mighty Romans guard the tomb made the resurrection of Lord Jesus Christ more believable.

Luke 24:1 - 11 [KJV] [1]Now upon the first *day* of the week, very early in the morning, they came unto the sepulchre, bringing the spices which they had prepared, and certain *others* with them. [2]And they found the stone rolled away from the sepulchre. [3]And they entered in, and found not the body of the Lord Jesus. [4]And it came to pass, as they were much perplexed thereabout, behold, two men stood by them in shining garments: [5]And as they were afraid, and bowed down *their* faces to the earth, they said unto them, Why seek ye the living among the dead? [6]He is not here, but is risen: remember how he spake unto you when he was yet in Galilee, [7]Saying, The Son of man must be delivered into the hands of sinful men, and be crucified, and the third day rise again. [8]And they remembered his words, [9]And returned from the sepulchre, and told all these things unto the eleven, and to all the rest. [10]It was Mary Magdalene, and Joanna, and Mary *the mother* of James, and other *women that were* with them, which told these things unto the apostles. [11]And their words seemed to them as idle tales, and they believed them not.

The Bible says that the women came early in the morning to the tomb, the Bible does not say that Lord Jesus Christ rose from the dead early in the morning. Remember that according to Genesis God's definition of a day is from evening to evening; therefore Saturday evening is the beginning of Sunday the first day of the week. Lord Jesus Christ most likely left the tomb Saturday evening instead of daybreak Sunday. The stone of course was rolled away so that Lord Jesus Christ disciples could get into the tomb and see that He had risen from the dead. The Apostles were not expecting to see Lord Jesus Christ alive again; therefore they refused to believe the truth of Lord Jesus Christ resurrection when the women told them.

John 20:3 - 18 [KJV] ³Peter therefore went forth, and that other disciple, and came to the sepulchre. ⁴So they ran both together: and the other disciple did outrun Peter, and came first to the sepulchre. ⁵And he stooping down, *and looking in*, saw the linen clothes lying; yet went he not in. ⁶Then cometh Simon Peter following him, and went into the sepulchre, and seeth the linen clothes lie, ⁷And the napkin, that was about his head, not lying with the linen clothes, but wrapped together in a place by itself. ⁸Then went in also that other disciple, which came first to the sepulchre, and he saw, and believed. ⁹For as yet they knew not the scripture, that he must rise again from the dead. ¹⁰Then the disciples went away again unto their own home. ¹¹But Mary stood without at the sepulchre weeping: and as she wept, she stooped down, *and looked* into the sepulchre, ¹²And seeth two angels in white sitting, the one at the head, and the other at the feet, where the body of Jesus had lain. ¹³And they say unto her, Woman, why weepest thou? She saith unto them, Because they have taken away my Lord, and I know not where they have laid him. ¹⁴And when she had thus said, she turned herself back, and saw Jesus standing, and knew not that it was Jesus. ¹⁵Jesus saith unto her, Woman, why weepest thou? whom seekest thou? She, supposing him to be the gardener, saith unto him, Sir, if thou have borne him hence, tell me where thou hast laid him, and I will take him away. ¹⁶Jesus saith unto her, Mary. She turned herself, and saith unto him, Rabboni; which is to say, Master. ¹⁷Jesus saith unto her, Touch me not; for I am not yet ascended to my Father: but go to my brethren, and say unto them, I ascend unto my Father, and your Father; and *to* my God, and your God. ¹⁸Mary Magdalene came and told the disciples that she had seen the Lord, and *that* he had spoken these things unto her.

John outruns Peter to the tomb, and out of respect he stops at the opening and looks inside, but Peter runs straight into the tomb without stopping. After seeing the linen clothes that Lord Jesus Christ was wrapped in without a body, John believed what the women had said about the resurrection of Lord Jesus Christ. Peter must have still had doubts because Mary Magdalene believes that somebody took the body away. The resurrected Lord Jesus Christ reveals Himself to Mary Magdalene and her sorrow turns into joy.

Matthew 28:11 - 15 [KJV] ¹¹Now when they were going, behold, some of the watch came into the city, and showed unto the chief priests all the things that were done. ¹²And when they were assembled with the elders, and had taken counsel, they gave large money unto the soldiers, ¹³Saying, Say ye, His disciples came by night, and stole him *away* while we slept. ¹⁴And if this come to the governor's ears, we will persuade him, and secure you. ¹⁵So they took the money, and did as they were taught: and this saying is commonly reported among the Jews until this day.

Before Lord Jesus Christ died on the cross and rose from the dead, He told the corrupt wicked religious leaders that they were not His sheep and that their father is the devil, now we know what that means; it does not matter how much evident there is to prove that Lord Jesus Christ is the Messiah and God the Son, they know the truth but are determined to suppress the truth from others so that they can continue to rule over the people.

Notes and Reflection:

Notes and Reflection:

Chapter 6: The Trinity.

The definition found in Webster's Dictionary says: Trinity *n . , pl .* -**ties** for2,4. **1.** the union of three persons (Father, Son, and Holy Ghost) in one Godhead, or the threefold per- sonality of the one Divine Being. **2.** TRINITY SUNDAY. **3.** (*l . c .*) a group of three; triad. **4.** (*l . c .*) the state of being threefold or triple.

The best example found in a Holy Bible commentary: Past + Present + Future = Time.

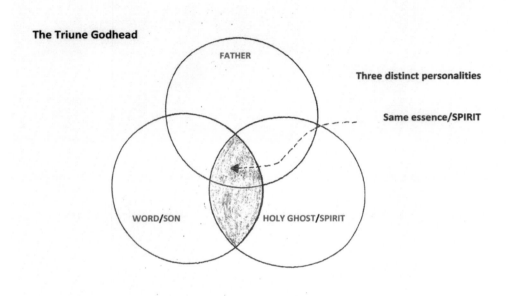

This is a list of names of God that are found in the Old Testament and New Testament that God uses to identify Himself to mankind.

Old Testament Names:	English	Hebrew
	God	El, Elah or Elohim
	LORD	Jehovah
	Lord	Adon or Adonai
	Almighty God	El Shaddai
	Most High	El Elyon
	most high God	El Elyon
	everlasting God	El Olam
	LORD God	Jehovah Elohim
	Lord GOD	Adonai Jehovah
	LORD of hosts	Jehovah Sabaoth

God – El, Elah or Elohim – is that name of deity which reveals Him/God as the strong, faithful One, who is one and yet, in some way not precisely defined, more than one; and who is to be trusted, obeyed and worshiped.

LORD or Jehovah – the distinctive redemption name of deity. (*The eternal self-existent One*)

Lord or Adonai – the Master of our service.

El Shaddai – "*the strong, sufficient One who gives.*"

El Olam signifies deity as "*the everlasting God.*"

Sabaoth means, simply, host, or hosts, but with special reference to warfare or service.

Seven compound names of Jehovah in redemptive relation to mankind.

1. **Jehovahjireh** – *"the LORD will provide."* Genesis 22:13,14

2. **Jehovahrapha** – *"the LORD heals."* Exodus 15:26

3. **Jehovahnissi** – *"the LORD my banner."* Exodus 17:8-15

4. **Jehovahshalom** – *"the LORD is peace."* Judges 6:23-24

5. **Jehovahraah** – *"the LORD, my shepherd"* Psalms 23:1

6. **Jehovahtsidkenu** – *"THE LORD OUR RIGHTEOUSNESS."* Jeremiah 23:6

7. **Jehovahshammah** – *"The LORD is there."* Ezekiel 48:35

The distinctive and final New Testament name *(not names)* **of God is:**

Father, Son, and Holy Ghost/Spirit. Matthew 28:19

"God" *(Greek Theos)* – a deity, the supreme Divinity.

"Lord" *(Greek Kyrios/Kurios)* – from Kuros; supreme in authority, controller.

The name that gives us the revelation of God incarnated in Christ *(the anointed One)* **is:**

Lord *(His divine name)* Jesus *(His human name)* Christ *(His official title)*

The Final Identity of God

Matthew 28:18 - 20 [KJV] [18]And Jesus came and spake unto them, saying, All power is given unto me in heaven and in earth. [19]Go ye therefore, and teach all nations, baptizing them in the name of the Father, and of the Son, and of the Holy Ghost: [20]Teaching them to observe all things whatsoever I have commanded you: and, lo, I am with you alway, *even* unto the end of the world. Amen.

Notice that "*name*" in the scripture text is singular not plural!

The FATHER   is viewed as the Head of the Triune Godhead.

The Son   is viewed as the Redeemer of Mankind.

The Holy Ghost/Spirit   is viewed as the companion and comforter of Mankind.

Chapter 7: The Seven Points of the Gospel of Lord Jesus Christ.

Gospel Explanation

Lord Jesus Christ was born of a virgin female, who had no sexual relationship with a man before His birth, and He lived a perfect life, without committing any sin._

Lord Jesus Christ is the only human being that's never sinned against God. He never did anything wrong, He never said anything wrong, and He never thought anything wrong.

Lord Jesus Christ is the Son of God and the son of mankind, which means that He is the <u>one</u> and <u>only</u> perfect infinite God - Man, He's one hundred percent human and He's one hundred percent God for eternity; <u>He's equally as much human as He is God!</u>

The Word, a member of the Trinity, entered into His creation and became a human being by being physically born through a woman who had never had intercourse, bypassing the sin nature that other humans are born with, because the sin nature is passed to others from the seed of the man.

Lord Jesus Christ died on the cross, and He shed His Holy blood, to pay the sin debt of every one of us who believes in Him. He never got married. He was born of a virgin woman and He experienced physical death as a virgin man.

Lord Jesus Christ willingly allowed His Holy Blood to be shed for the remission of our sins. The Human part of Him experienced the spiritual separation that we are born with while He suffered on the cross on our behalf.

Lord Jesus Christ was buried in a tomb, and He rose from the dead the third day according to the scriptures.

Lord Jesus Christ was physically dead for three twenty four hour days and then His body came back to life.

Lord Jesus Christ was seen alive, by His disciples at different times, for forty days <u>after</u> He rose from the grave.

Lord Jesus Christ met with His disciples after His resurrection and discussed some of His future plans with them and commanded them to spread/preach the Gospel.

Lord Jesus Christ disciples watched Him as He ascended into heaven in a Cloud out of their sight, and He sent the Holy Ghost or <u>Holy Spirit</u> on the day of Pentecost that came fifty days after the resurrection of Lord Jesus Christ, to indwell every believer from generation to generation until the church body is completed, and God the Holy Ghost give us the ability to have a close personal relationship with God in the person of Lord Jesus Christ.

The indwelling of the Holy Ghost/Spirit is our guarantee that we are saved and will spend eternity in Heaven with God. The Holy Ghost/Spirit is our spiritual connection to God. Lord Jesus Christ works in us and through us by way of the Holy Ghost/Spirit.

Lord Jesus Christ will return someday for all of us who believes in Him, the living and the dead, and we shall be with Him forever.

Lord Jesus Christ has promised to come back to earth and take every one who believes in Him back to Heaven with Him. Dead believers will be resurrected and those of us who are still alive will be pulled up into the sky to meet Lord Jesus Christ together. Our bodies will be changed into spiritual bodies and we will never die after that happens; we will live forever with God.

Notes and Reflection:

Why does God allow evil in the World?

Scripture Reading:

Exodus 34:5 – 7a [KJV] ⁵And the LORD descended in the cloud, and stood with him there, and proclaimed the name of the LORD. ⁶And the LORD passed by before him, and proclaimed, The LORD, The LORD God, merciful and gracious, longsuffering, and abundant in goodness and truth, ⁷Keeping mercy for thousands, forgiving iniquity and transgression and sin, and that will by no means clear *the guilty*;

Mark 10:17 - 18 [KJV] ¹⁷And when he was gone forth into the way, there came one running, and kneeled to him, and asked him, Good Master, what shall I do that I may inherit eternal life? ¹⁸And Jesus said unto him, Why callest thou me good? *there is* none good but one, *that is*, God.

Sermon Text:

There will come a time, in the life, of the believer, when he, or she, will have to make a crucial decision. Eventually we will have to decide, whether or not we will follow Lord Jesus Christ, totally and completely. But all too often, we choose to compromise with God. We say in our heart, or in our mind, *"Lord, I know what you want me to do, and I know how and when you want me to do it. But Lord, if I do it the way you want me to, the people will think I'm a fool, they will say that I'm confused. Lord I need to connect with the people. I know what they expect. What if?"* Any time we attempt to compromise with God, it's a clear indication that we do not have the right relationship with God.

The Bible speaks about a rich young ruler and his relationship to God, "**Matthew 19:16 - 22 [KJV]** ¹⁶And, behold, one came and said unto him, Good Master, what good thing shall I do, that I may have eternal life? ¹⁷And he said unto him, Why callest thou me good? *there is* none good but one, *that is*, God: but if thou wilt enter into life, keep the commandments. ¹⁸He saith unto him, Which? (*So Lord Jesus Christ dealt with him first, according to his relationship with man, many theologians call this the horizontal, man's relationship to man*) Jesus said, Thou shalt do no murder, Thou shalt not commit adultery, Thou shalt not steal, Thou shalt not bear false witness, ¹⁹Honour thy father and *thy* mother: and, Thou shalt love thy neighbour as thyself. ²⁰The young man saith unto him, All these things have I kept from my youth up: what lack I yet? (*Now Lord Jesus Christ will deal with him according to his relationship with God, many theologians call this the vertical, man's relationship to God*) ²¹Jesus said unto him, If thou wilt be perfect, go *and* sell that thou hast, and give to the poor, and thou shalt have treasure in heaven: and come *and* follow me. ²²But when the young man heard that saying, he went away sorrowful: for he had great possessions."

The message today is about knowing God better. The more we know about God, the more we will love Him. It's impossible to know God, and not love Him, because God **is** love. And if we love Him, we **will** keep His commandments.

The title of this sermon comes in <u>the form</u>, of a question. And the question is this, *"Why did God allow evil into the World, what is the reason?"*

Evil is something that affects all mankind throughout the whole World. We live in an evil world. Evil is something that we all have in common. No one is exempt from evil except God. All of us have experienced evil to some degree, we have done evil, and we have had evil done to us.

Therefore, how should we define evil? For the sake of this message, looking as best we can, from a spiritual point of view, let's say that evil is anything and everything, that's in opposition to God. <u>Evil is anything and everything, that's in opposition to God.</u>

Looking once again at the question: Why did God, allow opposition to Himself, to come into the World, what is the reason?

What do we mean by God <u>allowed</u> evil to come into the World? Logically speaking, if evil is in opposition to God, then chances are, evil would not be concerned about getting permission from God to do anything, unless it was absolutely mandatory!

The Bible tells us, "**Job 1:6 - 11 [KJV]** ⁶Now there was a day when the sons of God came to present themselves before the LORD, and Satan came also among them. ⁷And the LORD said unto Satan, Whence comest thou? Then Satan answered the LORD, and said, From going to and fro in the earth, and from walking up and down in it. (*The LORD did not bother with asking Satan why he was going to and fro in the earth, and walking up and down in it, because God is omniscient, all knowing, but the late Apostle Peter tells us what Satan is known to do in the earth. The Apostle Peter wrote in a letter,* "**1 Peter 5:8 [KJV]** ⁸Be sober, be vigilant; because your adversary the devil, as a roaring lion, walketh about, seeking whom he may devour:" *Satan means adversary, he is the chief evil spirit, the great adversary of God and humanity, and is known in the Bible by many names: the devil, the destroyer, the father of lies, I call him the author of confusion, and the Bible also calls him the evil one! Satan is the embodiment of evil, he is, and always will be, in total opposition to God*) ⁸And the LORD said unto Satan, Hast thou considered my servant Job, that *there is* none like him in the earth, a perfect and an upright man, one that feareth God, and escheweth evil? ⁹Then Satan answered the LORD, and said, Doth Job fear God for nought? ¹⁰Hast not thou made an hedge about him, and about his house, and about all that he hath on every side? thou hast blessed the work of his hands, and his substance is increased in the land. ¹¹But put forth thine hand now, and touch all that he hath, and he will curse thee to thy face."

The important thing to note here, is the fact that Satan said that God had put a hedge about Job. In other words, Satan could not touch Job unless God **allowed** him to do so. So, is this the reason that God allowed evil to come into the World? So that mankind would know that God is an almighty sovereign, all knowing God, and that nothing happens, <u>good</u> or <u>bad</u>, in the World unless God allows it? **No**, that's not the reason, it could be a reason, but it's not <u>the</u> reason.

What do we mean by the <u>World</u>? We see in the book of Genesis, "**Genesis 1:26 [KJV]** ²⁶And God said, Let us make man in our image, after our likeness: and let them have dominion over the fish of the sea, and over the fowl of the air, and over the cattle, and over all the earth, and over every creeping thing that creepeth upon the earth." So the World means the kingdom of humanity that was under man's dominion before the fall of man.

"**Genesis 3:17 [KJV]** ¹⁷And unto Adam he said, Because thou hast hearkened unto the voice of thy wife, and hast eaten of the tree, of which I commanded thee, saying, Thou shalt not eat of it: cursed *is* the ground for thy sake; in sorrow shalt thou eat *of* it all the days of thy life;"

This was the turning point in the order of things, when the evil one took control of the World and evil came in the World through Adam's disobedience to God.

"**Genesis 3:21-23 [KJV]** ²¹Unto Adam also and to his wife did the LORD God make coats of skins, and clothed them. ²²And the LORD God said, Behold, the man is become as one of us, to know good and evil: and now, lest he put forth his hand, and take also of the tree of life, and eat, and live for ever: ²³Therefore the LORD God sent him forth from the garden of Eden, to till the ground from whence he was taken." Is **this** the reason that God allowed evil to come into the World, to let mankind know that when we disobey God, there are divine consequences to our disobedience, or was it so that God could show His compassion for mankind? **No**, both of these could be **a** reason, but neither one of them is **the** reason.

Let's look at the Old Testament scripture that we read earlier, to see if we can find the reason there. "**Exodus 34:5 – 7a [KJV]** ⁵And the LORD descended in the cloud, and stood with him there, and proclaimed the name of the LORD. ⁶And the LORD passed by before him, and proclaimed, The LORD, The LORD God, merciful and gracious, longsuffering, and abundant in goodness and truth, ⁷Keeping mercy for thousands, forgiving iniquity and transgression and sin, and that will by no means clear *the guilty*;" in this scripture we see that God reveals to Moses that, not only is He a God of <u>love</u>, but He is also a <u>just God</u>.

Knowing that God is a just God, gives us hope for the future, when we understand that the wicked will eventually be punished for all the wrong that they do. And the reason for God allowing evil, to come into the World, is **hidden** in this scripture.

Those of us, who study the Bible on a regular basis, have learned from experience that the spiritual truths that are hidden in the Old Testament are revealed in the new. So let us look at the scripture from the New Testament that we read earlier.

"**Mark 10:17 - 18 [KJV]** ¹⁷And when he was gone forth into the way, there came one running, and kneeled to him, and asked him, Good Master, what shall I do that I may inherit eternal life? ¹⁸And Jesus said unto him, Why callest thou me good? *there is* none good but one, *that is*, God." "And Jesus said unto him, why callest thou me good? There is none good but one, that is, God."

Believe it or not, **this is**, the reason, why God allowed evil, to come into the World, so that when we say that God is good, we know what that means. It's not just an intellectual statement floating in our mind; it's far more than that, it's something we can **feel**, in our very being. God is good! If it wasn't for hot, how would we know what is cold, or if light was not day then how would we know the night?

God is a supernatural infinite being. We are finite creatures. We have limitations, but God to the best of our knowledge does not have **any** limitations. There's no way that mankind could ever through his or her intellect, figure out who God is. God has to reveal Himself to us. And that's what God has done for us, by allowing evil to come into the World. He has let us know that **He is good**! And we say it in various ways, God is good, God is good all the time, God is good every day in every way, ain't God good? **Don't** you know that God is good?

Now the question <u>is</u>: just how good is God? How do we measure the goodness of God? What can we use as a gauge, so that everyone can equally evaluate the goodness of God? Otherwise God's goodness would be relative to the amount of evil, one has experienced. Because God is good, He has provided a way by which everyone can equally evaluate His goodness.

The Bible says, "**Romans 5:8 [KJV]** ⁸But God commendeth his love toward us, in that, while we were yet sinners, Christ died for us." "**John 1:1 (KJV)** ¹In the beginning was the Word, and the Word was with God, and the Word was God." "**John 1:14 [KJV]** ¹⁴And the Word was made flesh, and dwelt among us, (and we beheld his glory, the glory as of the only begotten of the Father,) full of grace and truth." "**John 3:16 (KJV)** ¹⁶For God so loved the world, that he gave his only begotten Son, that whosoever believeth in him should not perish, but have everlasting life." The **<u>cross</u>**, is the measuring stick by which all mankind can equally evaluate the goodness of God.

Lord Jesus Christ, God the Son, who walked this earth as the infinite God-Man, 100% human and 100% God, died on the cross, and shed His Holy Blood for the sin debt of mankind. And He was buried in a tomb. He rose from death, to life again on the third day. He was seen alive by His disciples before He ascended to Heaven, where He is presently interceding on our behalf as an everlasting High Priest. Not only did He die to save us, but because He lives, He keeps us saved. He will return for us someday, and we will always be with Him.

God is real, God is good, and Lord **Jesus** Christ saves.

Notes and Reflection:

The Christmas Fable

John 4:21 - 24 [KJV] ²¹Jesus saith unto her, Woman, believe me, the hour cometh, when ye shall neither in this mountain, nor yet at Jerusalem, worship the Father. ²²Ye worship ye know not what: we know what we worship: for salvation is of the Jews. ²³But the hour cometh, and now is, when the true worshippers shall worship the Father in spirit and in truth: for the Father seeketh such to worship him. ²⁴God *is* a Spirit: and they that worship him must worship *him* in spirit and in truth.

2 Timothy 4:1 - 4 [KJV] ¹I charge *thee* therefore before God, and the Lord Jesus Christ, who shall judge the quick and the dead at his appearing and his kingdom; ²Preach the word; be instant in season, out of season; reprove, rebuke, exhort with all longsuffering and doctrine. ³For the time will come when they will not endure sound doctrine; but after their own lusts shall they heap to themselves teachers, having itching ears; ⁴And they shall turn away *their* ears from the truth, and shall be turned unto fables.

Introduction: Lord Jesus Christ told the Samaritan woman at the well that true worshippers must worship God in spirit and in truth. Most people in the World today do not know the truth.

The Bible says, "**John 18:37 - 38 [KJV]** ³⁷Pilate therefore said unto him, Art thou a king then? Jesus answered, Thou sayest that I am a king. To this end was I born, and for this cause came I into the world, that I should bear witness unto the truth. Every one that is of the truth heareth my voice. ³⁸Pilate saith unto him, What is truth? And when he had said this, he went out again unto the Jews, and saith unto them, I find in him no fault *at all*."

The Bible also tells us, "**John 8:12 [KJV]** ¹²Then spake Jesus again unto them, saying, I am the light of the world: he that followeth me shall not walk in darkness, but shall have the light of life." Because of Adam the created son of God disobedience in the Garden of Eden, all of mankind except Lord Jesus Christ (*does not have a human father*) is born in spiritual darkness, spiritually separated from God, with no knowledge of the truth about God or the things of God.

So, what is truth? The Bible says, "**Luke 4:4 [KJV]** ⁴And Jesus answered him, saying, It is written, That man shall not live by bread alone, but by every word of God." The Bible also tells us what Lord Jesus Christ prayed to God the Father, "**John 17:17 [KJV]** ¹⁷Sanctify them through thy truth: thy word is truth." Truth is the word of God that's found in the Bible; when we follow Lord Jesus Christ and His teachings that are found in the Bible then we are living according to the truth.

The Apostle Paul wrote a letter to his spiritual son Timothy, to inform him that some people are so deceived that they will hate the truth from God and embrace the lies of Satan the devil. They will be willing to believe in fables instead of the truth. The biblical definition for <u>fables</u> is false stories or myths.

The title of this message from God is, <u>Lord Jesus Christ and the Christmas fable</u>.

How did the Christmas <u>fable</u> December the 25th get started? According to a historian, it started during the reign of Constantine the professed Christian Roman Emperor (*A.D. 306 to A.D. 337*) who wanted a means of bringing pagans and professing Christians together for a more peaceful empire. The pagans already worshiped the Sun god on December the 25th and a decision was made during that time to declare that Lord Jesus Christ was born on the same day, to give all the people a common celebration in hope of unifying the people together. Constantine had successfully done this before by naming the <u>first day of the week</u> "Sunday" and also made it a holiday to unite his empire, the pagans kept that day in honor of the Sun and the Christians were already observing that day as the Lord's Day in honor of Lord Jesus Christ resurrection from the dead/grave.

True worshippers have to constantly make a choice between being politically correct and biblically correct. The atheists are trying to get rid of the Christmas celebration because they say that they do not believe in a God. On the other hand many professing Christians are trying to keep the Christmas celebration because they say that they believe in God. So, who is right and who is wrong? The professing Christians are wrong for trying to keep a lie about Lord Jesus Christ birthday that was started for political reasons as a true biblical reason.

Many professing Christians believe that Lord Jesus Christ was actually born on December the 25th, because this is what we have been told as children and they have never read through the whole Bible; God's truth to mankind, to see for themselves that the Bible never tells us exactly when Lord Jesus Christ entered into this World as a human being, nor does the Bible tells us to worship the birthday of Lord Jesus Christ. There are some professing Christians, including Pastors and other local church officials who seek to be politically correct; some even try to reconcile Creation and The Theory of Evolution.

Conclusion: Every true worshipper has the ability to worship God in spirit and in truth because we are indwelt with God the Holy Ghost/Spirit, also known as the Spirit of Truth; therefore we have an obligation to tell the truth and stop living a lie. We need to stop doing what we know is wrong, and also stop teaching our children lies about God in the person of Lord Jesus Christ. The Bible does not tell us the date that Lord Jesus Christ came into this World as a human being; therefore we do not have the right to choose an arbitrary day of the year to worship the so-called birthday of Lord Jesus Christ. True worshippers should seek to be biblically correct instead of politically correct!

Notes and Reflection:

References:

SCOFIELD BIBLE CORRESPONDANCE COURSE

Thru the Bible with J. Vernon McGee Commentary

Evangelism Explosion Ministry Teaching and Training materials

QUICKVERSE 2006 & QUICKVERSE 10 (*Bible computer software*)

Commentaries:

Jamieson-Faussett-Brown Commentary on the Whole Bible

Matthew Henry Concise

Commentary on the Holy Bible, A

Adam Clarke's Commentary on the New Testament

Adam Clarke's Commentary on the Old Testament

IVP Bible Background Commentary: New Testament, Ed. 2

Bibles:

KJV - The Holy Bible, King James Version

NASB - New American Standard Bible

NLT - Holy Bible, New Living Translation

ICB - International Children's Bible, New Century Version

NIV – The Holy Bible, New International Version

ASV – The Holy Bible, American Standard Version

NRSV – The New Revised Standard Version of the Bible

YLT – Young's Literal Translation of the Bible

NKJV – The Holy Bible, New King James Version

Printed in the United States
By Bookmasters